Until He Comes

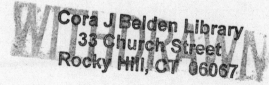

Until He Comes

A Good Girl's Quest to Get Some Heaven on Earth

K. Dawn Goodwin

G

GALLERY BOOKS

New York   London   Toronto   Sydney   New Delhi

Gallery Books
A Division of Simon & Schuster, Inc.
1230 Avenue of the Americas
New York, NY 10020

First Gallery Books trade paperback edition December 2011

GALLERY BOOKS and colophon are registered trademarks of Simon & Schuster, Inc.

For information about special discounts for bulk purchases, please contact
Simon & Schuster Special Sales at 1-866-506-1949 or
business@simonandschuster.com.

The Simon & Schuster Speakers Bureau can bring authors to your live event.
For more information or to book an event contact the Simon & Schuster
Speakers Bureau at 1-866-248-3049 or visit our website at
www.simonspeakers.com.

Designed by Renata Di Biase

Manufactured in the United States of America

10 9 8 7 6 5 4 3 2 1

Library of Congress Cataloging-in-Publication Data

Goodwin, K. Dawn.
    Until he comes : a good girl's quest to get some heaven on earth / K. Dawn
Goodwin. —First Gallery Books trade paperback ed.
        p. cm.
1. Goodwin, K. Dawn—Childhood and youth. 2. Women—Georgia—Biography.
I. Title.
    CT275.G55775A3 2011
    940.54'8173—dc23   2011036576

ISBN 978-1-4516-2712-1
ISBN 978-1-4516-2713-8 (ebook)

As this memoir is based on personal experiences from the distant past, events have been compressed and some dialogue approximated. Most of the names and distinguishing details have been changed.

To Mom, for knowing I could write it.

To Dad, for promising never to read it.

Acknowledgments

Thank you to my agent, Ellen Pepus, for finding me in the desert. Yours was the most sublime phone call ever received in the self-checkout lane of the Bremen, Georgia, Wal-Mart. Thank you to Amy Tipton, for working miracles that would do Jesus proud. Thank you to my editor, Megan McKeever, for getting it, and laughing, and changing my life.

Thank you to my sissy, for holding my hand—now, then, and always. Thanks to Mom and Dad, who kept me afloat when the ship was going down. If only every woman was so lucky. Thank you to my three babies, without whom I would never have woken up and taken a stand.

Thank you to Natlie, who taught me how to follow my heart. You always told me it would fly, so I guess this is really all your fault.

Thank you to Dawn—I'm sorry for ever doubting you. It will never happen again.

"Behold, I come quickly."

—REVELATION 3:9

Until He Comes

1 | The Girl from the
Show-Me-Yours State

"Therefore will I discover thy skirts upon
thy face, that thy shame may appear."

—JEREMIAH 13:26

When we left Missouri and moved to Connecticut, I didn't turn ugly right away. For a while, I lived with the peace that passeth understanding, because I still thought I was hot shit. Being ordained as the Child Prodigy of Attractiveness dovetailed nicely with God's two-pronged plan for my life: to share the Good News—and my goodies—with every sinner who crossed my path.

What I didn't know yet was that the Constitution State wasn't about godliness or prairies or the pioneer spirit; it was about loopholes in written contracts. It was about statutes of limitations, one of which was about to cinch closed on my head. On my ninth birthday, my golden shimmer of awesome would be snuffed out, and I would be as great with fugly as Mary was with the Christ child. Not even the Holy Spirit, who was like God's most highly anointed trial lawyer, would be able to put my humpty back together again.

But when I was seven, I was at the pinnacle of my career. Like the biblical Samson before me, all God's power was in my hair. And much like Samson, I attended second grade at Heritage Christian Academy in Shelton, Connecticut.

Before I left each morning, Mom would roll the sides of my hair with a curling iron, then scoop them back with a brush into feathered Farrah Fawcett dog ears. I'd cover up my face and she'd dowse my head with Aqua Net, a veritable force field of Pretty.

My siblings and I would load up in Dad's first company car, a blue 1980 Pontiac Grand LeMans, while he vigorously pumped the gas pedal in his polished dress shoes, trying to wake it from its eternal slumber. Over the din of flatulating backfires, Mom stood waving good-bye in a bathrobe, her breath frosting in the air.

On the ride to school, I fingered my crispy bangs and smoothed the navy pleats in my uniform. My skirt was the attaché case, and the top secret was that my yellow panties matched my blouse. Yet unlike my diary, it had no lock. Ah, the irony of the Christian girl. Yes, I was a *Christian*. I was *Saved*. The King of Kings, the invisible Captain of Team World, had not only redeemed me from eternal damnation but had ordained me with better hair. Basically, Jesus regularly borrowed *my* eyes to give you the once-over.

Dad pulled into the roundabout and I hopped out of the car, clicking my plastic heels across the cement. Like Victoria Principal's protégée, the top two buttons of my blouse were always left undone. I was little, but oh I understood sexy all right. I had to, since I was the main attraction in my classroom. Inside the front door, everyone turned to admire me, to fight over who would be the next to win a sleepover. *One at a time, girls, you'll all get your turn.* The director yelled "Action," and the extras began filling the background of my peaceful, nondenominational, evangelical uber-appealing Christian life. *Ding.*

In class, we stood at attention before the Christian flag and sang the morning doxology. Then we took our seats and Ms. White, in her modest shin-length tweed skirt and rounded bow collar, pressed pictures of lambs onto the felt board over the cutout of a burning altar. It was time to illustrate yet another bewildering obscure captain's log entry from the helm of the USS *Crazy,* aka the Holy Bible.

When the smoke from the sacrifice goes up, that's good, she said. When the smoke goes down, God frowns. See? In Genesis, Cain the farmer was smited because he burned veggies on the grill when God left *explicit hints* in the sky that He preferred to inhale the fat from dead animals.

I had a lot to learn about God.

The first thing was that He was highly passive-aggressive. For example, He didn't hate you per se, just your sin. To be clear: not you, just everything you do every day. He was also very jealous and known to overreact and, say, kill your whole family while leaving you dismembered, but just alive enough to wish you'd loved Him just a teensy bit harder. And, if His followers offered the wrong kind of burnt offering, or on the wrong day, or in the wrong order, or with the wrong ingredients, or if they tried to make it a nicer burnt offering, or if they forgot and slept in, God pretty much always reacted the same way. He devoured them with death. But tie your firstborn son to forty cubits of kindling and strike a match, voilà, the Almighty lifts an unplucked eyebrow. *Aha,* He'd say as you raise the trembling dagger over your newborn. *Now THAT'S more like it.*

But the Bible lesson learned was: follow through. Don't count on God manifesting like that, like He did with Abraham, breaking in with the Lord's emergency broadcast system to tell you *this is only a test.* Live by faith, even if it means jumping off the cliff like a lemming. Making horrific requests is God's way of saying He loves you. He just wants you to show some stick-to-it-iveness. Like with Jesus: there He was, hanging from nails, dying a slow tortured death per God's request, begging for mercy, but God so loved the world that He leaned into the ear of His only begotten son and whispered, *Don't be a quitter.* And whosoever believeth in that, Ms. White explained, shall have eternal life.

God was one hell of a heavenly Father.

And while buying me with blood was awfully nice of Jesus, He really couldn't compete with the other men in my life, like Tommy, or Tommy's twin brother, Timmy, and especially Jesse. Jesse was my age, supposedly a Christian, but that didn't stop him from longing to live in sin with me. Once, he'd even whispered something in my ear about "grabbing a nightcap," which I imagined was like taking Communion naked inside his sleeping bag. The best of both worlds. I loved Jesse because he excelled at a) planning questionable trysts, and b) smoldering with jealousy.

He was especially mad at me today because I'd shared a Bible with Tommy. And then got stuck reading the end of Genesis chapter two. Blame God.

"And she shall be called Woman, because she was taken out of Man," I'd read.

"Very nice," Ms. White interrupted, marking the page.

"That is why," I continued, enjoying the sensual purr of

my voice, "a man leaves his father and mother and is united to his wife, and they become one flesh."

Ms. White: "Very nice, you can stop there."

"Adam and his wife were both *naked* and they felt no shame."

"Ms. Goodwin, that is enough."

Startled, I moved my fingertips across the page, where they came to rest on Tommy's hand. He blushed and Jesse glared at me hard from a few desks down.

"What?" I mouthed.

He immediately began writing me a note.

As punishment he was going to meet me after school in the cafeteria and kiss me. Hard. But I wasn't worried. Being ravaged had nothing to do with Satan really. It was merely the gravitational pull of my own worldly charms, bestowed on me so I could better lead sinners to the light. Kind of like the way Christ bought us with blood; only I used Bonne Belle.

Jesse was waiting for me in the dark behind the last cafeteria table, fists jammed into his tan polyester pants. I approached and stood in front of him, feeling guilty and electric all at once. I let my book bag slide seductively to the floor.

"Hi," he said, looking so serious he was almost in pain.

"Hi, Jesse."

"Do you like Tommy?"

"No."

"Good."

Then he gave me a quick peck with dry, soft lips and ran out the cafeteria doors into the fluorescent light of the hallway. I watched him flee, wondering if we were closer now. I picked up my bag, realizing this must be how the Bionic

Woman felt about the Million Dollar Man. All womanly and bionic and stuff. I shoved open the double doors and headed outside to join the pickup line, chomping at the bit to testify before my Christian BFFs. They of course gathered around me, eager to hear anything I had to say. I soothed their wide-eyed fears, took their calls, offered advice about all the pivotal milestones I'd already high-jumped. It would take them years. It was so adorable, how much they all wanted to be like me. *Aw*.

At three o'clock Mom picked up my older brother and sister and me in the roundabout. It was a long, boring, woodsy drive home, and also the template of my entire budding universe. Along the way, I reminisced over all the many amazing signs God had left for me. The house that was the same color as the boogers I so loved to eat, the ditch where Mom had once pulled over so I could puke up chicken noodle soup, the four-way stop where I realized that Lemon Meringue was my favorite Strawberry Shortcake doll, and the hill where I realized that all these events had one mysterious common thread—the color yellow. My life was fascinating.

Once home, I ran upstairs and slipped into my room and out of my Heritage Christian jumper. There was a green paisley cover on my dark-varnished bunk bed. Mom had arranged my favorite stuffed animals on the pillow just so. On one wall were the Curious Kitten and Orphan Annie posters that I'd gotten at the book fair. On the other wall was a centerfold of Cheryl Tiegs, posing suggestively with a bobcat. Cheryl was a gift from the old Italian grandma who lived across the street and who demonstrated various decadent behaviors not likely endorsed by the puritanical matrons of the Bible, such as feeding her German shepherd vanilla ice cream in a dog bowl. She thought since I was a good Christian girl, and didn't have a dog, I might like this half-naked, sexually objectified supermodel, and she was damn right. Every day as I unzipped my uniform, I admired Cheryl and her lean denim hips, her hair the same wild texture and ash-blond color as bobcat fur. Someday I was going to transmutate into that, only, you know, slightly more New Testament. I'd wake up one morning and have long, blond curls that were 100 percent dandruff-free, like Christie Brinkley in the Prell ad. I'd be making out with men in tuxedos, one after the other. And oh, my colossal tits. The profile of my symmetrical D cups, aching to be freed from my soft but tight sweater, would have hot guest stars swooning. They'd fistfight each other over the chance to draw my bath.

In Bible class at school, sometimes I'd color in Jesus's beard and start daydreaming. Dang. He was kinda hot too.

Needs to work on self-control, read the note from Ms. White. It was the second warning that year.

"What does that mean?" Dad would ask, loosening his tie. All he wanted was the nightly news and a hot supper; instead he got my ominous report card comments and me, marinating in my naturally improper juices. "Bloody well better start controlling your 'self,' so help me."

"Daddy, you're not supposed to say 'bloody,' " I warned.

He looked back, muzzled. "Yeah, well. It's absolute nonsense."

Things had gotten complicated since we'd left Springfield, Missouri, and moved to Connecticut. Mom and Dad had started their family in the Midwest because it was closer to Mom's family, and also to Jesus Himself. Sure, Dad was a full-blown, pinkie-ring-wearing, blue-blooded Brit, but when he laid eyes on USDA choice Mom, he immediately opted to spend the '60s not wallowing in free love but converting to the Church of Christ so he could legally fornicate with her. Enter us: a crossbred litter of God-fearin' Amerikins.

Looking back at faded snapshots, I always pictured Missouri in the early '70s as a Norman Rockwellish kind of place, where kids came complete with cowlicked hair the color of white corn, adorably wholesome little Midwestern twangs, and souls as pure as prairie snow. Missouri folks were kindly, the cashiers and clerks trustworthy, the lines short. Townsfolk had their priorities in order and likewise drove their vehicles in a reasonable manner.

But when Dad got a much-needed promotion to corporate HQ in Connecticut, my parents had packed up the station wagon, said good-bye to the relatives living at Mom's homestead, and made the stalwart trek eastward toward the double mortgage of the American dream. As hundreds of miles of pastoral scenery gave way, a panorama of bleak, polluted, and crumbling turnpike rose up around us like the Red Sea. Brake lights flared and salt-caked cars bullied each other through one narrow connector after another, leading us onward to the inverted promise of New Canaan.

As we crossed our new state line, Mom read the names aloud from her map: *Bridgeport, Saugatuck, Trumbull.* All the Connecticut towns along I-95 had the poetic assonance of being punched in the gut. And although the map assured us that the ocean was somewhere close by, it was never visible above the sea of grimy tailpipes and towering black-tipped smokestacks that nested in the endless tangles of electrical relay stations. Abandoned brick factories with smashed, toothless windows loomed over empty, trash-filled lots. Mom's knuckles grew whiter and whiter around the thin, hard steering wheel.

Soon she would learn that the natives of Corrupticut were a greatly pissed-off people, biologically ill equipped to get into heaven, should Jesus happen to drop in unannounced. Soon, she would grow to accept that the snow never melted, the prices were sky-high, and the jackass stealing her parking space at the A&P was her next-door neighbor.

When we'd first arrived, I was too young for school, so I spent a lot of time watching Mom from the backseat as she drove around Gridlockington from errand to errand.

"Time to drive to Armpiton," she'd say with mock cheer before loading me in the car. The New England peddled in Christmas cards was apparently for suckers. But it was the salespeople who truly broke her. After making a withdrawal from a teller at the Connecticut Bank of Assholes, or maybe buying a bra from the clearance rack at Condescending Bitches boutique, Mom would retreat to the car and sniff over the steering wheel, dabbing her eyes with a crumpled Kleenex.

"How can they treat people like that?" she'd say aloud, to no one. "How?"

"Um, did you get me a lollipop?" I'd ask, at home among my people.

She pulled a green one out of her cash envelope, handed it back to me, and turned the ignition.

"Fairfield County," she growled.

I fingered the wrapper, my eyes wide. It was the closest thing to a cuss word I'd ever heard her say.

It wasn't just Mom who took it hard. The tougher side of Connect-a-cut quickly sawed off the last nub of innocence belonging to my twelve-year-old brother. He walked to his new school, which was just around the block from our new house, and promptly ran home screaming before lunch. Booth Valley Elementary, probably named for John Wilkes Booth, shone like a beacon to all offspring of the tired, poor, and yearning to be in organized crime. Big bro's endearing Midwestern twang and Ozarks T-shirt, and also Mom's insistence that he continue to play a wussy violin, put my beloved big bro at the top of their list for a mock whacking. Death threats were put on our family cat, and my parents were forced to sign away Dad's newly acquired salary hike. All three of us kids were going to Heritage Christian Academy.

Oh, goody, I thought at the time. Parochial kindergarten was the perfect place to start amassing my fan base. And after school I could spend my free time carrying out the Heritage Christian mandate: Save. More. Souls.

Since our new neighborhood was kind of bad, I had a lot of shaming to do. And by bad, I mean they clearly weren't as Christian as us. We had lots of Frankies and Ralphies and Johnnys, who liked to throw my metal tricycle, with me still on it, into the curb in front of our house. More than a few pieces fell off. Johnny towered over me.

"Say, 'Kiss my grits,' " he commanded.

"Kiss my grits," I echoed, wondering if this was how sinners made friends with Christians. A kind of ritual hazing, to make themselves feel worthy. My brother stood motionless in the background as the crew of kids snickered. *No sudden movements,* he was thinking, *and we'll all stay alive.*

"No!" Johnny barked at me, "say it in here!" He spit a wad into the gutter near our feet. I looked down through the grate at my reflection in the murky water.

"Kiss my grits," I called, starting to like these strange heathens more and more.

"Now. Spit," Johnny told me.

I did, and wiped a long string of saliva from my chin.

"Know what your new name is?"

"Am I Flo?" I asked excitedly, because *Alice* was one of my favorite shows.

"No. You're Puke. We'll call you L'il Puke."

Satisfied, Johnny returned to bullying my brother. I dragged my busted bike up the driveway, handlebars in one hand and wheels in the other, brimming with indignation. Dear Jesus, what exactly was going on here? How could I possibly save these boys? No one wanted to hear the Good News from a messenger known as Li'l Puke. Please. Hope they liked going to hell.

One day we came back from church, which we attended a minimum of three times a week, to find eggs smashed against the back side of our house.

"Buncha punks," Mom said in a low voice, surveying the damage. "That Johnny."

The trajectory of the shells pointed to Johnny Moretti's house next door. Johnny's dad had a fleet of broken down Cadillacs hidden in his window-high weeds. He'd been living there since long before we came along and must have been pleased when they bulldozed his backyard to put in our quaint two-story Tudor. To show his appreciation, he kept a pack of bipolar Dobermans pointed toward our house, choking on the ends of their chains, legs quivering, and tendrils of pink foam swinging from their muzzles. For Mom, it was one more reason to want her money back. And her old life.

While she made phone calls to get a ten-foot-high

privacy fence built, I prayed for Christ to protect us with His giant disembodied hand, roughly the size of our backyard, for Johnny's dad to mow his lawn, and for God to save all kittens from the mafia.

In the meantime, I would spend more time indoors with the TV.

When I was seven we had had only four channels, but it was enough. *Guiding Light,* which of course was about us since it was based in a town called Springfield (Missouri, duh), helped fill in most of the blanks left by the Bible. Most of the time I could figure out whose side God would be on. But when it came to *sleeping together*—bare shoulders rolling in satin sheets, whispers about Jack finding out—it was still anyone's guess.

"He *won't* find out," she'd promise her lover, as the camera zoomed in for another sticky kiss. My older sister, Kate, who was ten, rolled and flopped with me on the carpet in front of the TV, screaming, "Turn around! He's right there! He's in the doorway, duh!"

Then our eyes glazed over as blue liquid was poured into maxipads, over and over and over. *I feel secure thanks to Kotex,* said the lanky blonde, smiling as she leaked and soaked up more Windex than ever before. She was the same woman whose elusive *freshness* got her lost in the meadow. She tap-danced over the scent of her Downy sheets and was finally rendered retarded by the crispetty crunch of her potato chips, the shocked whites of her eyes still burning on the screen after the fade to black.

Next was *Little House on the Prairie:* lean, honest, hard-workin' Midwestern pioneers with healthy bosoms, muslin dresses, and wholesome pies cooling in the windows of sturdy log cabins. More moral victories in an hour than one could count. Pa Ingalls flashed Ma that gorgeous smile as he hitched a team of horses, sweating through his unbuttoned shirt.

"God'll provide, darlin'," he'd always say. "Don't you worry yer pretty head."

Occasionally, while fixing the roof or building a barn or saving the town, Michael Landon would break a rib and have to go shirtless, his sublime tan pecs wrapped in gauze. Kate and I stared at his body, openmouthed. But the lily-white Ingalls daughters, unfazed by his comparative swarthiness, huddled 'round Pa in their bedclothes and nightcaps, smiling as he played the fiddle by firelight. Pa always fingered the strings all wrong, out of sync with the dubbed lullaby. But it made us love him more somehow.

"We'll always have each other," Laura Ingalls said as the camera panned away through the window.

"Oh corny corny *corn*," my sister sang, doing a handstand against the couch.

I didn't know what she meant exactly, but if ever there was a quintessential word for *Little House on the Prairie, corny* was it. From Laura's bucktoothed smile to the town shucking contest, this was the embodiment of pure unadulterated corn. Corn that completed me.

But by far the best part was that the TV writers could always be counted on to come up with tantalizing plotlines that the real Laura Ingalls Wilder would never have put in her book. Like the episode about the girl whose boobs got too big for Walnut Grove.

"Bind yourself good, child," croaked her old man, alluding to her ample breasts, which were clearly making all the children in the schoolhouse insane. "Tighter, girl!" he warned, wiping drops of sweat from his long red nose.

The girl went into her room with a roll of gauze that Doc Baker had probably given her and began binding up her tits over an old-timey undershirt. Meanwhile, the townie boys peered in her bedroom window, hoping to catch a glimpse of that rack. She was usually so good about keeping the shades drawn, but conveniently not today. Good times!

If it were me, I daydreamed, if I were lucky enough to have boys peeking in *my* window trying to see *my* tits, I wouldn't bind them up so quickly. I'd strip down totally nude and bend over real slow to pick up my Bible. Then I'd pause to study Leviticus with my splayed buttocks resting directly against the window, or maybe my bare chest, criss-crossed like an ammo belt, with my ginormous nipples popping through. I'd probably have to just lie there, innocently pondering what to do as the boys busted in one after the other to take turns feeling me up.

Unfortunately, no one was looking in my window. I ached with jealousy.

Someday they will, I promised myself. *Someday.*

Meanwhile, back in Walnut Grove, this girl's simmering mammaries had every innocent Christian man and woman in town trying to think of something else. They were doing a pretty good job, until the writers of *Little House on the Prairie* dropped a bomb on them, in the form of a mask-wearing sexual predator who crept predictably through the woods. As our well-endowed teen strolled through the meadow picking flowers, he snuck out, put a gloved hand over her mouth, and pulled her into the brush. Later, she stumbled home to confess to her even creepier old man.

"He grabbed me," she sobbed. "He held me down, and

he . . . he . . . !" *Da da da DA DA*. The background orchestra became deafening, to remind us it was best to be vague and quietly picture what had happened.

"No one must know of your shame," her father growled.

My imagination exploded. I knew what had happened. I knew. He had forced her to *sleep with him,* only this time in the bushes instead of under lavender satin sheets. And with a clown mask on. I didn't know what this meant, but it was very exciting and I wanted to try it.

After the commercial break, during which Kate trotted to the kitchen for snacks, the girl was already pregnant.

"IT'S BACK ON!" I screamed.

She ran back in with her hand in a box of Trix. "What did I miss?"

"He grabbed her," I explained. "He held her down, then he . . . Da da do DA DA DA!" I played the loaded crescendo on my air violin. "And now she's PREGNANT!"

I dug feverishly into the box of cereal and shoved a handful in my mouth, hopping up and down. Fruity cereal somehow maximized all the pleasure.

We stared, mesmerized, as Pa cornered his son Albert. He was the last male seen with Ms. Tightly Bound Jugs. They'd been carving their names in the old oak tree.

"Did you?" Pa asked his son. "Albert . . . did you . . . ?" His chin was quivering.

"Look, his chin is quivering," Kate said.

"I know!"

"Pa . . . no . . . I never!" cried Albert, running out the door. Then, when it seemed like the weepy background orchestra couldn't possibly climax any further, the pregnant girl tumbled down a ladder in the barn and perished without a squeak. The rapist was shot with no notable ramifications, other than a whole lotta satisfaction, and Pa and Albert were again robust, innocent, and socially well adjusted.

But I was utterly ruined, left to ponder the majestic adventure and sweeping tragedy of Big Boobs.

Once the credits rolled, anything in our house that was remotely breast shaped—oranges, tennis balls, decorative ashtrays—spent some time under my shirt. I'd cat-walk back and forth, trying to decide the right proportion for my future body. Best in show always went to Mom's plastic L'eggs panty hose cups, cracked in half and stuck under a cardigan. For the chance at lopsided torpedoes like those, oh, there were no words. The Holy Grail.

But since my prepubescent chest remained devoid of drama, I made a mask out of a paper plate and pretended to be Catwoman.

I ran outside and into the neighborhood, lurking in the trees, hissing at imaginary demons, leading an army of invisible cat people with my intrepidness and raw power. But I'd lift the plate up off my face long enough to tell passing kids about God's love, how Jesusdiedfortheirsins, and to ask if they wanted to go to church with me, which usually frightened their mothers.

So I turned my attentions to Ricky, the little boy who lived across the street. He was manageable. He was probably named Rick until he moved to Connecticut, where by law all boys' names must become adjectives. You could tell by looking he was going to end up browning on Satan's rotisserie. Ricky and his little brother Marty didn't wear uniforms or go to Heritage Christian like we did. Plus: they swore. And peed everywhere. Anywhere, anytime, and with amazing distance.

"Have you asked Jesus into your heart?" I asked him one day. I was standing in his backyard, looking up at him as he climbed into his tree house.

"Have I what?" he said, like it was the stupidest thing he'd ever heard. "No."

I followed behind him, in short shorts and a halter top that showed off my pale distended belly. Just to show him my after-hours, non–Heritage Christian body.

"Do you go to church?"

"On Easter," he said, hoisting up onto the plywood platform. "And Christmas."

"You only go then?" Ricky's soul: sullied by years of poor attendance, like the blackened lungs of his chain-smoking dad.

"Yeah. But my dad doesn't have to go, just me and my mom. And Marty." Then predictably, Ricky reached for his fly and whipped out his small fleshy penis so he could pee on me. Again.

"Wanna bet I can squirt that bird in the eye? The one at the top of the streetlamp?"

While I tried to make this compute, his dad tossed a smoldering butt in the grass a few yards away and Ricky spot-drowned it without looking twice. I dropped off the ladder to feign covering my eyes.

"Ew! Did you get any on me?"

"Want me to?" He wiggled his hips and the yellow stream arced over my head.

I screamed, running out of range. "Stop it!"

"But I'm not done," he told me, filling up an empty soda can at the top of the platform.

I was getting tired of playing the shocked onlooker. Why did Ricky get to have all the fun? It was time to get mine. So I marched to a pile of cut logs a little ways back and dragged a line through the dirt with my toe.

"Hey!" I hollered. "This is the *girls'* bathroom. And you can't come in!"

I crouched down out of sight in the buggy mulch, wondering if I dared.

It's okay, I thought. *I told him not to look, now the rest is out of my hands. Right, Jesus?*

I slipped my hands inside the elastic of my shorts just as Ricky's footfalls crunched the leaves.

"Ricky!" I startled, looking up. "You can't come in!"

"Go ahead." He grinned, craning his neck to watch. "I'm not looking."

"Oh," I said, catching his drift. "You promise?"

"I promise," he said, lowering his voice, crouching down closer. "Do it. I won't tell."

And just like that, I was totally and completely hooked.

Relieving myself outdoors with sinners in my neighborhood became more than a slippery slope; it was a luscious avalanche of sin that swept me into the world of glorious, off-color role playing. As soon as I got home from school, I switched personalities. I stuffed my shorts with grass and leaves, so I made a crinkly sound when I walked, and headed across the street. I found Ricky as usual, peeing upside down from his rope swing.

"Noah's son Ham saw his dad's wiener," I told him halfheartedly, "and God had to kill the whole town for it. So don't say I didn't warn you."

"Isn't it time to use the girls' bathroom?" he asked.

"First you have to remove my diaper," I replied coyly, patting my overstuffed crotch.

Ricky zipped up, grabbed a plastic sword that was lying on the ground, and forced me onto the family picnic table like a sacrifice, where I told him I was giving birth to the Christ child and needed to be tied up and cut open. Ricky found some twine and then got to sawing.

"Hey!" Ricky's mom shouted through her kitchen window. "God damn it! What are you kids doing?"

"Mrs. Dunner?" I sat up, grass and leaves spilling out of my unbuttoned shorts. "God said in Matthew 5, verse 34, 'Swear not at all.'"

"Oh, yeah?" she said, dragging on a Virginia Slim. "Was there a verse in there that said, 'Tramp ye my boys, not at all'? Now get off my new table and play nice."

The next day I was back, with little ripped up pieces of paper in hand.

"Tickets to the strip show," I whispered. "In the basement. At my house."

I didn't want it to come to this, but sometimes, y'know what, the devil just takes over, makes us do really really fun things we hate. Sad but true. The way it worked was, you just sort of escorted the little miniature Jesus out of your heart—like maybe into a waiting room near your intestines—and focused on the Bible verses that promised God would forgive anything if you prayed hard enough. *Anything*. That was a direct quote, pretty much. You just had to remember to pray later, much later, after the dirty deed was already done dirt cheap.

"Ricky, come on!"

He was working with an electric sander in his garage,

always playing with band saws and car jacks and chain saw engines while his four-year-old brother mixed cement nearby.

"Marty!" he hollered to his brother over the growl of the motor, "hit this board a couple times with the nail gun!" Then he paused to consider me through safety goggles.

"The stripper has to take everything off," I told him. "*Everything.*"

How did I know what a stripper was? Oh, I had an idea. I was a high-powered magnet for scraps of information.

My mom had taken us once to a lady who ran a hair salon out of her kitchen, and there on her coffee table was a stack of glossy magic otherwise known as *Playboy.* Kate and I had hovered around the massive powder-laden breasts, covering our mouths with the kind of prudish shock that would've made Caroline Ingalls proud. I longed to peek inside, but Jesus paralyzed me in His loving force field and held me fast, then the lady came and gathered them up in a flurry.

"Sorry, I'm not used to having kids around," she told my mom.

Mom gave us a loaded look, *Can you believe how tacky?* But oh, I longed to meet more tacky people like her. People who had stacks of *Playboy*s lying around the couch like *Better Homes and Gardens.* Christians, on the other hand, did their best to ignore Song of Solomon, which was the only book in my Children's Bible with no illustrations, but it was packed with innuendo about pillars, gazelles, and spices wafting out of people's gardens.

Ricky summed up my shapeless form and agreed to the strip show.

"Okay. Break time."

It had to be done in a hurry, a pusher waving addicts into the back room to do the deal. I gave them a two-for-one price and pranced back and forth on the back of the couch, humming a burlesque tune, kicking off pieces of clothes on the downbeat. Once it was all off, I swear I heard Jesus weeping, and my song seemed more like the high-pitched squeal of a boiling crab, or perhaps the inner tube of my soul deflating on Satan's tack. I jumped down and hightailed it to the closet, covering both sides of my ass.

"Show's over!" I said, slamming the doors closed in Ricky's face.

He was having a good laugh, eyes gleaming, mistaking my escape into the closet as part of the act. He set to banging the door down, trying to pry it open with his fingernails, until a light flicked on at the top of the stairs and my mother asked what was going on.

"Hide-and-seek," he called back.

"Please don't bang on the closet doors. Where's my daughter?"

"Don't know," Ricky called back, covering his little brother's mouth.

She's in here, my conscience cried out. She's stripping naked and doing incredibly exciting things that will bring great shame to her family.

Who knew this inner, ethereal orb known as the conscience could hurt so bad? The next day, I opened my dresser drawer to find the same sailboat halter top I'd worn as a stripper. There it was, neatly washed and folded by my mother. All innocent and waiting to be worn again.

Something wrong? It asked me.

I backed away, stunned and reeling. It was a lump of Satan's kryptonite.

At night, the shame blossomed. *People's butts,* my feverish thoughts moaned over and over, *people's butts are so sinful.*

The parts you want to show most are the ones you have to work hardest to cover, explained the Lord, as He placed a pair of peach-colored buttocks on the felt board altar. *Bind it tight, child! Bind it!*

God said He'd forgiven me, but clearly it wasn't enough. I couldn't forgive myself. Guilt loomed around every corner, dragging behind me everywhere I went, like my Fisher-Price turtle-on-a-string. I was *bad.* I was a *bad girl.* How could I purge this ache in my chest, this heavy noose of sin around my neck, and get back to being awesome and good again?

The more I thought about it, the more I realized that everything I'd been taught, including the Bible, *Little House,* and *Guiding Light,* pointed to one thing: dirty secrets could be absolved only when confessed to the one person you wanted to tell the least, and who probably also did not want to know.

That would be my dad.

"I did something," I mumbled to him one night, after lights-out. "I did something *bad* with Ricky."

"Who's Ricky?" Dad asked.

He was sitting on the edge of my bed, no tie, but still in his dress shirt. Since he was always away on business trips to the far corners of the earth, he often had to be refreshed on the cast members of my life.

"The boy across the street."

"Oh." He yawned. "Okay."

"I took off my shorts . . ." I continued, the words stuck in my mouth. "I took them off."

"And . . . what? He saw your underpants?" Dad, always the optimist.

"No," I said.

"He saw your backside?" So upbeat and calm, like the pilot on the intercom as the plane goes down.

"My front side too," I squeaked, hoping if I put a touch of wonder in my voice—golly, Pa—perhaps it would go down easier.

"So, you showed Ricky your bottom?"

Bottom! Yes! Such a silly, wonderful, all-encompassing word, we could just as easily have been discussing the bookcase, the bottom shelf, the bottoms of our hearts.

"Yes, my bottom," I said, letting the tears flow so he would take it easy on me.

"It's okay," came the bewildering answer. "But boys and girls need to keep that private."

Okay? I thought. *Okay??* It must be Dad's new job. His senses must be dulled by the high blood pressure. Or maybe my nudity still qualified as cute, like the little girl on the Coppertone bottle. So we said prayers, and I added a silent one that God would help me with the last fruit of the spirit, the dreaded self-control. Please keep my Fruit of the Looms covering the fruit of my loins, in Jesus's name, amen!

In the morning, there was a letter from my dad, who now believed his prolonged absences had totally screwed me up. The note taped to my bunk bed had a heart and an arrow through it, telling me he would never stop loving me.

Clutching my pass, thanks to my possibly underinformed and secular-leaning father, I was back to enjoying life one day at a time when Nathaniel, whose desk faced mine at Heritage Christian, told me he would show me his ding-a-ling if I showed him my cooter.

"My what?"

"You know what," he said.

Sure, Ms. White had left the classroom for a minute, and Jesse was out sick, but I wasn't going down the road of naughty fun and excitement again. Oh, no. Not that. I had a reputation here. I was popular and respected. But I had tasted sin and wanted more. Just a little bit. Just a smidge.

"You go first," I whispered. I looked around to see if anyone else suspected. My girlfriends were distracted, coloring in their workbooks at other tables.

Under the desk I saw nothing, just Nathaniel's dark blue polyester knees, his hands fumbling in his shadowy crotch.

"Did not!" I said, sitting up.

"I did too. Look."

"No!"

"You have to show me yours now."

"Mine?" I said, intrigued. I had had a dream about this very situation, not long ago, where I was standing in class and dropped my drawers for everybody. I was filled with a sensation like I'd peed my pants, but way better. I woke up to dry sheets. It was definitely not the Holy Spirit.

"Just for two seconds," I told Nathaniel, "and that's it." While Jesus gathered up His scrolls and headed for the hills again, I stared directly at the board, hooked my arms into my dress, and you know, just sort of aired things out a bit.

"Okay," I whispered. "Look now."

Nathaniel disappeared under the table and came up with a dull thud, knocking his head. His face had changed, dropped. Hmm. Maybe he didn't have sisters.

"I saw it," he said. And then: "I'm telling."

I watched him get up and walk to the door to await the teacher's return.

"Nathaniel, please don't, *please don't*," I mouthed to him from my chair, the horror thick as tar. Oh, Jesus. Help me.

Nathaniel's face was pained, his clip-on tie askew. Moses stood at his back with a skewer of heathen babies and a pissed-off flaming bush. *Report her, ya little wussy.*

"I have to tell," Nathaniel whispered back to me. "I have to."

"*Please . . .*" I whispered. "*No.*"

"What's wrong?" asked my friend Jenny, alarmed by my crumpling, reddened face. "Something's wrong," she alerted my devoted crew. "We need to see if she's okay!"

"It's nothing," I whispered back to all their staring faces, shooing them away. "Nathaniel's just being mean."

"You need me to punch him?" Linda asked, twisting over her chair, loud enough so he could hear.

"Be nice to her or else," threatened Mia, "her boyfriend will be really mad."

"She is *bad,*" he snapped back at the girls, and my heart sank. They looked at me, questioning, unable to identify my sin, blinded by my flawlessly feathered hair.

It was too late. The teacher returned, the class hushed, and Nathaniel walked over to her desk, confessing quietly, shifting in his loafers, the whites of his eyes flashing as he tilted his head in my direction. No one could hear what they were discussing, but I knew the end was near. If only I was the girl who gets held down in the woods, I thought, and gets forced to lift her skirt. Then everybody would feel sorry for me. But no, I was the girl who begged passersby to please *undress me with your eyes.* My life was an episode too perverted even for *Little House.* Now *my* chin was quivering. My neck bent over my construction paper cross, which I no longer had the life force to paste together. I sat and awaited the loving axe of my Savior.

Ms. White asked aloud if I would please stay after class to speak to her. What would I do? What would I do when she referred to my bottom? My *privates*. Maybe she would read me a Bible verse. I'd get a U for Unsatisfactory. An H for Hellbound.

"Were you being inappropriate with Nathaniel?" she asked, after the room had cleared. That word. Worse than *unsaved* or *unclean*—anything was better than such a particularly willful and offensive brand of queer as *inappropriate*.

"No!" The tears threatening. "No I didn't. Nathaniel *lied*." Tension ebbed from Ms. White's face. Lying was definitely more tolerable than anything involving panties or a penis.

"Well," she said, "I'll have to call your parents about this."

Dread seized me. I had no escape; I'd have to lie. Lie like I'd never lied before. I would lie so hard I would reverse the past, turn the world back on its axis, like Superman.

When my mom got the call, I hid behind the couch, soothing myself with the striped upholstery pattern. Blue, tan, brown. Blue, brown, tan. Little fuzzy lines in between. I traced them with my finger.

"What is this about Nathaniel?" Mom asked me after she hung up.

"He lied about me," I said, casual-like.

She stood there looking down at me.

"I don't know why he lied about something like that," I said. "That is so disgusting."

I explained my side of the story, the one where my bottom was in a deep, ageless sleep, swaddled in privacy and correctness. I was practically perched around Jesus's feet like a pleasant robotic virgin on a commercial for heaven.

A parent conference was called. Dad would attend as my emissary.

Before work one morning, he came into school early in his suit and tie, smiling at me and my classmates in the hallway as he passed. We were standing around in the foyer before the bell. His smart camel trench coat turned down the hall and disappeared into Ms. White's lair, where no children could go until seven fifty. Dad was so tall and dapper. This impromptu visit would've been another excuse to bask in self-worship, if only it was Bring Your Parent to School Day. Instead it was Become an Unwitting Pawn in the Evil Web of Lies Concocted by Your Pleasure-Seeking Daughter Day. But I could just hear him, brandishing his shiny black hair and British accent like a magic wand.

Ultimately, I was right. The teacher believed me, because really. What kind of girl would take off her panties under the desk? Not one like me, who had a trophy for the most memorized catechisms in her class. Everyone concurred: it must be dirty, crotch-obsessed Nathaniel. He was swarthy, and his dad didn't sound a thing like Prince Charles.

During our daily Bible studies, Ms. White had once told our class that if we balled up our fist and pointed it at hell, hell being the floor, then it could block Satan from tempting us. Like a shield. For months post-Nathaniel, I'd been knuckling the devil into the throw rug, but my lie still weighed like a stone in my chest: 2–0, Satan in the lead. My righteousness was hemorrhaging.

I'd see something funny on TV, but before I could laugh, my sin reared its head.

Remember how you lied? Hmm, life's not so funny now, is it.

I'd be setting up a music concert for my Smurf collection in the living room, and there it was: a ticking time bomb in my chest.

You showed him your butt and lied.

No matter how seemingly sweet and innocent my day was, it was but a smear of pink icing on a mountain of impacted crap. I would have to come clean. Otherwise hell, like Pat Benatar sang, really was for children.

"Mom," I blurted out one night before she went back downstairs. "I lied about Nathaniel. I really did show him my bottom."

Mom considered me, then turned around and kept going.

"This again," she said. "You know what? I don't want to hear it. Honestly."

I trailed behind her, wiping my tears, relieved that the truth had set me free, and that Mom was not quite godly enough to refresh my teacher on the facts.

"Don't come crying to me," she called back, heading into the kitchen, "because I don't want to hear it." She snapped on rubber gloves to scour at the sink, a metaphor for my indiscretions. *Connecticut,* she scrubbed. *Is a fine place.* Scraping harder. *To raise children.*

I backslid only one time after that. With Mia, one of my many adoring little fans. At her house one day, we got naked from the waist down so we could slap our naked butts together to the Bee Gees. We would do this while jumping on the bed in her room with the door locked, squealing and laughing like hyenas. Originally, this had been my brilliant idea, but Mia, who believed I was God's gift to Christianity, caught on quickly. It wasn't long before she asked for naked butt slapping by name.

"Let's *do it,*" she'd whisper in my ear, so close I could feel her warm breath on my cheek. She giggled with excitement as we undressed in her room.

But something was very wrong. We were having too much fun. Which meant we were probably being *tempted.* I paused to consider the sunlight filtering through her white curtains. It wasn't golden and peaceful, it was God's X-ray vision. He was watching us. Mia's warm, smooth skin bumping up against my naked ass wasn't soft and sublime like I'd first thought; it was more like Satan stomping on the Holy Spirit's head with steel-toed cowboy boots. And the Holy Spirit wasn't just air, according to my Bible Workbook—the Holy Spirit was actually God's pet dove! There were feathers everywhere. Invisible bloody feathers! All because I had been tempted by yet another bottom!

"Gotta stop," I told her, getting down off the bed, pulling on my corduroys, and pointing my fist squarely at hell. I looked up at Mia's flushed, disappointed face. "I can't do it anymore. It's . . . bad."

"Oh," she said, brushing her hair out of her eyes, wondering when it was that I'd become such a boring, uptight turd.

Right then, as I was zipping up my fly, I decided I should be a doctor. It was a rightful end to all this silliness. I would get a license, and then I could peek and peer at all my patients' privates while they held still and counted ceiling tiles. I wouldn't be grabbing them and holding them down in the woods. I'd merely be within my rights as a professional.

Until such time, I would hog-tie my sinful impulses, gag them and sit on them and hum and count to a hundred. I would not be like Lot's wife in Genesis 19:26, who committed the worst sneak peek of all time, and *kapow,* God turned her into a bouillon stir stick for the instant soup of God's chosen people. I had to stop getting carried away. The Bionic Woman wouldn't go around lifting her skirt, if she had one. She was too busy being husky and beautiful and fighting bad guys. And Bathsheba, she was only being herself—an obedient maiden of God—when her nudity won her the king of Israel. It was completely by accident that he saw her in the bathtub. Great women were *chosen* to be spied on. The trick was, let your loveliness exude effortlessly, like radon gas, and biblical bridegrooms would somehow fall unconscious out of the sky.

If I could be like them, minding my own business, saying no to temptation, rejoicing in my modesty, then maybe one lucky day when I least expected it, when my beauty reached its Brooke Shieldsiest breaking point, some handsome man would come along and grab me, hold me down and, you know, *da da DA*. Then we could get married and never wear clothes again.

2 | Girl-on-Girl Socks

> "They shall bow down to thee . . . and
> the dust of thy feet they lick up . . ."
>
> —ISAIAH 49:23

I loved Ms. Lyons because I believed her name meant she was part jungle cat, like the guy in *Manimal*. And also, she was the butchiest, most enigmatically sexy-looking, Christianiest dyke I'd ever laid my seven-year-old eyes on.

Ms. Lyons was our gym teacher at Heritage Christian. She was in her twenties, had a short brown mullet, a wiry, athletic build, and wore anklets that had little red pom-poms above the heel. Maybe I loved her because of her socks. Nothing else could really explain my need to get close to her. I was sure to mention to her how much I truly, wholeheartedly *loved* her socks. Loved them. But the only way to adequately convey it was to accost my mom until she bought me several of my own matching pairs.

They have to be *red*," I explained to her in the apparel section of Caldor, sweating blood from my eyes. "They have to be *red*. Red like *Ms. Lyons's*."

At gym, I ran to show Ms. Lyons my feet, dizzy with excitement. The problem was, once in front of her, I couldn't think straight. I knew she was beaming down at me with that incredible toothy grin, but I was afraid to look directly at her, for fear I'd melt under the searing heat lamp of my own admiration.

"Ms. Lyons," I squeaked dryly, turning to show her the backs of my ankles. "Ms. Lyons . . . look."

"Oh, I like your socks!" she said, smiling big. She was so *nice*.

Then I sprinted away as fast as I could, to line up for dodgeball. Being in the same gym with her made my body manufacture its own biological heroin. Pure elation. Even if I wasn't looking at her, just knowing she was within range completed me. I threw the ball for her. I ducked for her. I got hit in the head, well, because I sucked, but I knew Ms. Lyons could tell it was for her.

Sometimes, when my class passed by the gym on the way to music, I'd break out of line so I could peek in the rectangular windows of the gym door, tugging on the handle so I could stick my head in.

"Hi, Ms. Lyons!!" I'd call into the echoey rafters. And she'd stop whatever she was doing to wave.

Sometimes it wasn't enough to just love her socks. I had to organize my complicated thoughts in my diary.

Ms. Lyons is my favorite teacher.
She has pom-pom socks.
She is nice.
I really really really like Ms. Lyons.

Sometimes I'd write a note and sneak it into her hand as we were filing out of gym class.

Dear Ms. Lyons,
You are the nicest teacher. You are my favorite.
I love your socks! Will you wear your red ones
tomorrow? I'll wear mine too.

Handing her the folded note choked me with embarrassment, but gave me the same feeling as meeting Jesse in the back of the cafeteria. It eased the yearning, then made me cross-eyed for more.

The next day, when I saw her red pom-poms peeking out of her white sneakers, I had a small seizure. Careful not to swallow my tongue, I ran up to her, breathing hard. My posse of girlfriends followed behind me, because they had taken my cue and gotten pom-poms too. I glanced back at them and secretly rolled my eyes. Please. This had nothing to do with fads. This was connection. This was devotion. Go away.

"Hi, Ms. Lyons," I said, approaching slowly, each step full of meaning. "I wore them."

"I wore mine too!" said another girl.

"Very nice, ladies." Ms. Lyons laughed.

I beamed up at her, twisting, unable to think of anything to say, besides, *okay bye!*

At the end of second grade, I learned that she was moving away, and I realized it wasn't just her socks. It was her. The shape of her body, the feel of her eyes on me, it all made me unspeakably happy, and unbearably sad.

Dear Ms. Lyons,
   I can't believe you are moving away. I don't
want any gym teacher but you. Please give me your
address so I can write to you. I'll miss you. I will
always love your socks. That's all for now.

That summer, she wrote me back. I held her letter in my hands. Yellow legal pad. Blue ink. Her hands had slid across this very same page. I smelled it, looking for a clue. She told me she missed me too, that I was a great girl, and to keep writing. And she was still wearing her socks.

It took me a long time to get over Ms. Lyons. She had a special place in my heart. A place that was only rented out months later, to Connie, my new babysitter. She was seventeen and didn't wear any socks. But she had curly hair and supple, tan thighs. And I could hardly wait to start sitting on them at story time.

3 | Relocating to Babylon

> "Come hither, I will show thee the judgment of the great harlot."
>
> —REVELATION 17:1

In third grade I found out we were moving to Avon. I'd asked if it was Avon like the makeup lady. But no, it was Avon the picturesque Connecticut suburb named after Shakespeare's birthplace, and makeup was quite beneath the well-educated ladies of the town. Instead they favored preppy bobs and year-round ski tans.

Avon was the lush, woodsy kind of place where Volvos ran free, where people came for the PhD per capita schools but stayed for the golf. Their ethnicities were many but their dream was simple: that they might raise nightmarishly good-looking children who would someday conquer other children with their expensive clothes, popularity, and scholar athlete accreditations. And, in the process, never have to run into one single black person.

I was shocked that I had to leave Armpiton. At Heritage Christian, seven out of the eight girls in my class adored me, and all the boys had secret crushes on me. When I walked into the classroom, they clustered around me, hurrying to be the first to save me a seat. Days before a field trip, I'd have to perform triage on all the incoming requests for bus partner. Sometimes Jenny wept if I didn't pick her. Sometimes Linda tried to make me jealous by inviting Mia over, poor thing. Any sleeping bag without me in it was destined to be kinda lame. But how could they help but covet me, with my proclivity for light sinning and imaginative seminudity? Their worship fit perfectly with the Kotex commercial of a life I knew I was meant to have. Ah, these poor lower-middle-class Christian Connecticut girls. Their baseline of prudishness and lack of access to a Conair curling iron made it so easy for me to feel like Smurfette in a colony of eunuchs. Like Blair on *The Facts of Life*.

But now, my hit show was getting dropped in its third season. This did not fit with the paradigm of my hair getting blonder and more powerful, so I figured it had to be like an unexpected promotion. My old life had simply reached its expiration date, and somewhere new friends were waiting with bated breath to behold my beauty and accept Jesus as their one true Savior. I was about to level up.

But first I had to break the news to my harem. One afternoon, I called an impromptu recess meeting behind the portable classrooms.

"I have something to tell you," I said to them, pausing to look dramatically off into the distance, like Charles Ingalls sometimes did. "I'm moving away . . . far, far away. To Avon. And, once there, I'm . . . going to go . . . to *public school*."

Linda sucked in her breath and Mia clasped her hands over her mouth. Jenny shuddered. It was agreed: they couldn't waste time. They had to pray right then and there.

My pretties. They were the most perfect studio audience an eight-year-old could ask for.

"Mom says it's one of the best public schools in the state," I offered, as they joined hands and bowed heads.

"Dear Jesus," Linda prayed, ignoring me, "please don't let her get tempted by Satan and stuff."

We closed with "in Jesus's name, amen," which was like hitting the Send button, then went to hang upside down on the monkey bars so the boys could see the shorts we wore under our jumpers. Making chitchat with our skirts about our ears—this of course was my idea.

"In Avon, school doesn't start until eight thirty," I continued to brag, though it was harder to talk with the blood pooling behind my eye sockets. "And you get thirty minutes for recess . . . and a real cafeteria . . . with like gourmet food."

"Are you allowed to pray?" asked Mia over the edge of her skirt.

"No, the other kids won't love Jesus like we do, but we can wear jeans as tight as we want to, and there's no rule on how long your shorts have to be." I flipped to the upright position, to see if the boys were watching. "It's kind of a trade-off."

At home, in my soon-to-be-obsolete bedroom, I paced around the braided rings of my soon-to-be-obsolete throw rug. It'd been the perfect track for racing my Hot Wheels, especially the black Trans Am with the firebird on the hood. Transammy was my favorite car because, like me, he was on fire and always finished first.

Where are we going? he asked me, talking through his miniaturized metal grille.

"Well," I whispered back, winking into his headlights,

"let's just say we won't need this ratty old rug where we're going. Think plush. Think wall-to-wall carpeting!"

The rips in the rug looked back at me sadly.

Oh, it said. *Guess you two don't need me anymore. Guess they'll just throw me in the cold lonely dump where no one will love me anymore.*

"No," I reassured it, kneeling down to pat it. "You still matter, Ruggy."

Tears blurred my eyes. The cameras panned in from above. There were so many who needed me, so little time.

The movers were coming, so I layered my stuffed animals in cardboard boxes, explaining to them that it was going to be very exciting, and they would be safe. An *adventure,* I told them and winked cheerfully. But as I closed the flaps, I sensed their panic, the crowded darkness closing in around them, no hope of escape. *No air!* I flung the top back open and their little plush mouths sighed with relief.

You saved us! they cried.

"Calm down," I scolded, channeling the biblical Abraham, leading a temperamental horde into the desert. "Have ye no faith?" They looked back at me, silenced by the heroism in my voice, and my stunning grasp of the Old Testament. I stuck imaginary oxygen canisters inside their box and closed the lid.

"There," I said. "We've got it under control. Just calm the heck down."

I only used the *h*-word when I meant business.

To deal with my growing anxiety, I came up with an imaginary black horse named, well, Blackie. I did this because Laura Ingalls on *Little House on the Prairie* had a black horse too. Named Bunny. Only hers was real. But whatever. I'd watched that episode repeat for years, envying

Laura as she clutched the leather reins, and Bunny's hooves thundered across the golden, sunny meadow. Together they won the race against Nellie Oleson and her thoroughbred, not because they were better—but because they were the good guys. They had simple things, like God and Pa on their side, not money and the mercantile. Oh, I needed me some of that, now more than ever.

Everywhere I went, so did Blackie. I led him around on a rope. Onlookers would never guess, unless they noticed my right hand clenched into a fist and cocked strangely to the side as I pulled his lead. At night I tied Blackie to my bedpost, brushed his imaginary mane, fed him imaginary oats from an imaginary burlap bag.

On moving day, I rode him frantically in circles around the backyard. I galloped him over to Ricky's house. I rang the bell and Ricky came to the door and blinked at me with those sunken eyes, peach fuzz on his top lip.

"I'm moving," I said. "To *Avon*."

"Yeah, duh," he said, without a trace of anything. I waited but only heard the TV blaring in the background, the smell of his house wafting out onto the front stoop.

"I'm going to public school too," I said, meaning, *I'm one of you. Only more special.*

"Oh," he said. "Okay."

Whatever, I thought. I had to feel bad for him. His life would be so much emptier without me peeing in his yard all the time.

Avon was an hour north. On the virgin voyage to our new, upgraded digs, I sat in the back of the station wagon, facing backward, watching the steep, woodsy hills wheel by and the white highway lines flash out from under the car. Mom's muzak was piping through the back speakers, the DJ over-enunciating WRFG in his stuffy baritone. My brother Kyle rifled through his cassette tapes and put on his headphones. The engine pushed and pulled. My stomach rose softly into my ears. My eyebrows filled out with a sickly, dull ache.

"Put the window down," I whined, stretching out to disperse the queasiness.

"She says put the window down," Kate hollered to the front, scooting away from me.

"She all right?" asked Mom from the passenger seat.

The back window inched down and sucked out some of the hot vinyl air, but Dad was busy weaving expertly through traffic, left, right, brake, lurch. Just parallel to the highway a river frothed and flowed, heading back in the direction of our old house.

Take me too, I thought.

Before loading up for this drive, Kate and I'd been building a tunnel house out of all the extra cardboard moving boxes. It snaked like a gopher tunnel from one end of our basement to the other. We'd filled our bowls with leftover coleslaw and crawled back inside our cardboard breakfast nook to eat it. I was trying not to think about all that pale, mayo-covered crunchiness now, or recall smelling it, or the fact that food existed at all. But I could see my fork resting in the empty bowl, pieces of cabbage stuck to the sides.

It'll get better, I told myself, pulling on the top of my hair to try and pop off my head, anything to relieve the ache. I tried to find something cold to look at. *Just need fresh air.* I squeezed my face with my hands till I left red marks, hoping to override the pain with more pain. It was getting worse.

"Pull over," I moaned, scooting forward on my seat, suppressing the telltale hiccups.

"She says *pull over.*"

"Pull over," my mom barked to my dad, who was going ninety in the far left lane. "Pull over NOW."

Dad swerved toward the shoulder, and I filled the floor with partially digested coleslaw.

By the time the car stopped, I felt great, but the family was miserable and clawing for clean air. I watched Mom through the window, wiping my puke off the floor mats in the weeds. She was gritting her teeth as the wind from passing traffic buffeted her hair into her face. It was an omen of things to come.

True, I'd just barfed my guts out, but when we finally pulled off onto our new exit ramp, I was optimistic again. Big things were in my future. Although in Avon, everything was teensy. The gas station signs were dwarfed, encased in brick and yellow pansies. Banks and high-end jewelry shops were disguised inside little cottages, next to what looked like a diorama of a period colonial village. We passed an old saltbox in town with working black shutters and poured glass windows.

"Honestly, Kyle, take off your Walkman and be a part of the family," said Mom. "Look at that quaint little New England inn!"

"Discount Tire," Kyle read, squinting at the sign.

"Oh," said Mom. "But it's still quaint!"

The outdoors were just as cozy: a huge driving range with a sweeping view of a scenic ridge in the distance. Real horses meandered inside miles of white rail fencing. Cute little steepled churches were nestled tastefully amid the rolling hills.

"I still smell puke," said Kate, as we turned into our new neighborhood.

The street sign read simply BLUESTONE. It had evolved

beyond trappings like St. or Rd. or Dr. The houses were tucked back behind tall trees, designed—at long last—to deliver maximum Christmas card value.

My sister and I climbed out of the car and up the stone steps of our new, empty house, caressing each detail. We opened doors and cupboards with awe, as if we'd never seen working hinges before.

"Look!" I screamed inside a drawer. "A nook . . . *for the cereal*!"

Nooks were good. I needed nooks. Safe little worlds that no one knew about, hidden inside the crannies of the bigger, scarier English muffin world. I made my way through the massive rooms and called Blackie to my side. I couldn't wait to get outside and ride him around and around and around in circles, beating his shiny flanks to a froth.

"Hold on, Blackie," I whispered. "Gotta check out the upstairs."

My brother looked out the kitchen window, expressionless.

"Yeah, hold your horses, Blackie," he said. "Oh, wait. You are a horse. Silly me."

At Bluestone, everything came in twos. We had two fireplaces, two sinks in the bathroom, two doors leading into Mom and Dad's room. But it wasn't just a room—it was a master suite with an audaciously purple Jacuzzi in the corner. I perched on its lavender carpeted steps, amazed that I had evolved past mere bathtubs. Now I could fit all my Sea Wees AND their lily pad–shaped sponges AND their floating lagoon, with enough room left over to swim underwater with goggles in cramped circles. I had arrived.

Of course I didn't realize I would never be allowed to fill the Jacuzzi to capacity, on account of the water bill.

Because despite all the Italian marble in the foyer, and all the walnut trim in Dad's new company car, our family's unspoken moral compass was Mom's well-worn house clothes and hefty coupon organizer. I knew better than to ask if we'd struck it rich. It was my job to be exuberant and appreciative, assuring them I had not been spoiled by this, our amazing—but possibly revocable—stroke of good fortune.

On my first day of school that fall, I made my entrance onto the blacktop of my new school: Bubbling Brook Elementary. Mom snapped my photograph before I turned toward the playground where all the kids were milling around waiting for the first bell. I waved good-bye and shuffled past the strange faces, clutching the straps of my empty backpack. I waited as my awesomeness exuded, as my magical curb appeal took effect on the heathens.

There were so many of them.

While I waited, the first thing I noticed was Avon girls. They weren't playing freeze tag or weaving cats in the cradle; they were huddling in circles with their backs turned, as if for warmth. It was not cold out. They were receiving some kind of social heat from the center, chattering and giggling and ignoring everybody else. A preppie-looking blond boy approached a girl-huddle, and the amoeba of their bodies opened to engulf him.

"Drew! We love you!" they squealed. "Did you love tennis camp?"

"Yeah," said Drew, "but oh my God, I hate my mom!"

As they laughed hysterically over this inside joke, the whites of their eyes flashing like sharks in chum, I noticed that these girls were so . . . tan. Tan in a way that made them cool. I looked at their skin, then their shoes, then back at my own. Their denim jackets had GUESS tattooed on the pocket, like a press pass. Monogrammed book bags. It's no big deal, said their fingers, twisting around locks of lightened hair. Doesn't everyone get their braids done in St. Thomas?

Ten minutes ago, I'd been reasonably certain that I was the golden child. But suddenly, I was average. Worse: I was invisible. Until I stared a little too long and was detected. A redheaded girl with a severe fringe of bangs turned to annihilate me with a glance, spot-checking me for country club readiness and overall elegance of carriage. She hit me with the loaded pronoun.

"Can we . . . help you?"

I backed away, and this attracted the pity of some homely-looking nice girls, like stray dogs to fresh carrion.

"Hi, what's your name?" one asked me. *Oh no,* I thought. *Her clothes look as dumb as mine.* But I knew what she was thinking: *We can't leave the new girl all alone. That would be mean, and mean would be unthinkable for nice girls.* Which was why I couldn't tell them out loud that I wanted to hold out for better friends. My edict was to be supernice, to wallow in shared niceness with man and God, who was also supernice, and to continue smiling nicely while sinners made haste upon my morning execution.

We lined up to go inside to get our locker assignments. I'd always dreamed about this moment. Having my very own locker. I would pad it with carpeting and drill in shelving, fill it with cozy nooks and safe crannies where my stuffed animals could dwell in peace and safety. But that dream had never included living adjacent to Niles, a boy terrorist in a pink alligator shirt.

"Nice jacket," he choked, slamming his locker closed. "What are you, Bozo the Clown?"

Apparently my charms, much like my fashion sense, had been cultivated by Jesus Christ and were appropriate for small, private school audiences only. I was no longer the Lord's sexiest spokeswoman. I was more like John the Baptist, staggering out of the wilderness and into a soirée already in progress. Bits of locust guts dangled from my beard. The patrons fanned away my stink.

I felt it was best to ignore all of these shocking slap downs, because Jesus hath said: *turn thee thy other cheek.* Soon, mine were flipping like a roll of toilet paper. Jesus forgot to point out that, when you turn that much cheek, sinners tend to wipe their asses with your face. Niles thought he'd died and gone to the all-you-can-eat power-trip buffet. I found him waiting for me every morning by the classroom door, as if an insult delivered early ensured him good luck all day.

"Oh, those shoes are cool," he'd coo. "Where'd you get them, Dorks R Us?"

His sidekick leaned in to examine the nondesigner tag sewed to the butt of my jeans.

"FabGirl?" he read and sputtered. "What's up, *fag girl*?"

Moments before I was assigned a "helper" from the Newcomer Club to show me the ropes, I prayed—harder than I'd yet prayed in my young life—for God to please let it be someone Niles respected. *Please, dear God, set the tone for my life. Please. I beg of thee.*

But God had a nice girl in mind, someone He approved of, someone with creased slacks and no friends. As she escorted me around that first week, I tried to pull away from our shared space so that maybe my head would be mistaken for another body. Every time she smiled at me I smiled back, and my Christian love recoiled and shriveled.

Then Drew, a really cute jerk, discovered my Michael Jackson notebook with the King of Pop posing on the front in his gorgeous yellow shirt and bow tie.

"Oh my God," he moaned, holding it up. "She likes *Michael Jackson*?"

A hush of disbelief went over the sea of white faces in my classroom.

He tossed it to another boy as if it had bit him.

"Gross!" he yelled.

I watched the stripping happen in slow motion, shaking in my boots. I stooped to gather my fallen papers, wondering if they were planning on killing me next. Instead, the boys dragged my notebook to the corner, where they devoured it whole. Drew stretched out on the floor, trying to get more comfortable as his friends huddled over his shoulders. Occasionally, they found a really juicy page where I'd written God knows what, and their muffled laughter crackled like gunfire. I looked up to see their squinty faces leering back at me, like having a front-row seat to my own disembowelment. But I didn't want to stare at them—that would be so rude—so I quickly looked away.

How had I been programmed to like things Avon people hated? I was eager to accept punishment and make changes to my clearly unkempt personality. Panicked, I dumped my Heritage Christian sandals, ripped the labels off my myriad of Michael Jackson accessories, and frantically prayed for something, anything with Benetton on it. In Avon, Benetton was like sacrificial blood. If you had it over your doorway— or on your back—you pretty much got a free pass from anyone, even the Angel of Death. I looked at my pants and felt an icy chill. They were the polar opposite of Benetton. They were a direct threat to my life.

The clothes, the clothes, *the clothes*—this was my non-stop high-pitched mental frequency. Around my head, cuffs and buttons and hems all danced like visions of a sugarplum massacre. Cute was the Antichrist. It had to be cool, it had to be expensive, it had to resemble MTV or *Young Miss* magazine, it had to pass muster with the popular girls at the caramel center of the playground huddle. What normal nine-year-old girls did before bed, I did not know. But I was obsessing before a full-length mirror, cat-walking every possible shirt-pant combination, each accessory like a colored wire on a bomb only Jesus or MacGyver could decode.

There wasn't exactly a whole lot to choose from in my closet. With the new and improved house came a hefty-hefty mortgage, leaving me to create the latest fashion out of whatever was handy. I mined every closet in the house for ideas and accessories. Maybe my brother's plaid button-down with my sister's red leg warmers? If only I could take in Dad's cardigan on the sides and make it a little more, y'know, Christian Lacroix. If only I could sew like Molly Ringwald, making complete ensembles out of scraps of fabric that I'd pulled out of my ass. The only thing I could do was safety-pin my pants into slightly different shapes. This required zero know-how and zero time, and usually stayed together great. As long as I stood still all day. At recess, I wasn't sure which was worse—the fact that I was the last kid picked for the kick ball team or the fear that a safety pin would come loose and reveal my pants as bell-bottoms.

"What are you doing to your clothes?" Mom asked

while I pinned myself up for school. I was desperate to make my loose, stretched-out turtleneck appear tight to my neck. I had to make my jeans peg-legged. I had to pin extra pins inside the cuff in case a pin gave way. I looked back at Mom, who was wearing a shirt she'd had since 1972. There was no way to explain.

I stared at myself in the mirror. Niles had now worked out a time-share in my heart with Jesus, so it was becoming harder and harder to figure out where the imparted Truth was coming from. *You are ugly,* he sneered when I put on my new red Reebok moon boots.

No I am not! I could be a trendsetter.

Yeah. A trend for ugly.

I wore them to school anyway, to see if I could. I chewed my nails to nubs. I stuck a magnetic mirror inside my locker, so when Niles started in, I could have something to turn to, and blame.

"Oh, my God," said Niles, dry heaving. He grabbed as many of his buddies as he could, bringing them over and pointing under my desk. "Look."

Ignore them, ignore them, ignore them, I chanted.

Later, in the lunch line, I stood behind Benjamin, a freckle-faced kid with bed head and ketchup crusted on his upper lip. He turned around to stare at me.

"Hey," he said, "you're kinda ugly."

It was like prophecy. It was like a snap of lightning, draining the life and color out of everything I was, everything I'd ever been, everything I would never be again after that moment, amen.

"Thanks," I whispered, shocked, thinking *no.*

"You're welcome," he said.

I couldn't fathom the bluntness. Any Christian knows

that when you meet someone who's ugly, you don't tell her. You just change the subject or something.

I wasn't ugly. I was still me. I still had potential to be fabulous, right?

I needed to look in a mirror immediately, but there was none handy. I was blocked in by a stream of faces holding their lunch trays. What about her? What about the white girl with the Afro, or that one, with two rows of front teeth? Why hadn't Benjamin called them ugly? Why only me? What had happened? My future glared back at me like a Dead End sign, erasing my purpose, blotting me off the map.

I picked up the first of many plastic lunch trays as Ugly Girl. Behind the counter, a lunch lady was taking a box cutter to a parcel marked Grade-B Food. Second rate, like me, like the cafeteria food I so enjoyed. I put my Jell-O next to the gray beefburger, kept my eyes on the floor tiles, and disappeared into the din.

Popular Avon girls were mean, but popular Avon boys made them look like fluffy kittens. These boys were a living turd sandwich of unadulterated misery. They'd even formed their own elitist club, *the Johnnies,* whose charter was to police and reinforce the female pecking order, each and every business day.

Ginormica, our teacher, was like their very own wet nurse. Tired and slow moving, she spent most of that school year sitting behind her desk resting her chin on her hand, digressing from spelling so she could fawn over the social hierarchy. Ashley, the most popular girl in our grade, was her absolute fave.

"Isn't she just cute as a button?" Ginormica gushed, as the rest of us homely forgettables turned obediently toward Ashley to admire her.

Since Ginormica had trouble moving around, she always had an errand that someone needed to run for her. But before choosing Ashley to do it, she wasted a lot of time asking for volunteers.

"Who wants to take this to Mrs. Jones in second-grade?"

Cue the sea of raised hands and the eager but futile chorus of *oo! pick me!*

"Ashley, c'mere, kiddo," she called out, letting all the air out of the room.

As Ashley stood to take her rightful place above us, Ginormica beamed.

"You're just so pretty." She smiled.

"That's because her mom's on the board," someone whispered.

The board? I had no idea what the board was, but I pictured a wooden ledge on a shelf none of us would ever be able to reach.

"Why don't you go with her, Carrie," Ginormica continued. Carrie was one half of a set of identical twins in our grade and thus had been granted automatic celebrity status. She didn't even seem to have a pulse, or need one. She and her twin Christy were born and bred for the sole purpose of escorting Ashley on her errands to the lower school. I watched them both leave, caressing their meticulously preppie turtlenecks with my eyes. There were no seams along the backs of their necks where a safety pin held their heads in place.

I spent a lot of time staring at Ashley from afar, wondering why every man, woman, and child was under her spell. It wasn't just her or her propensity to be both friendly and cold at the same time—that was easy—or the fact that there was nothing interesting enough about her face to make fun of. The magic ingredient seemed to have more to do with her choice in bodyguards.

Like Ellie.

Ellie was by far the most vicious female ever documented in the wild, and on the playground, she never left Ashley's side. Sure she was lanky bordering on awkward, but her cool was always resurrected by her ability to shoot pure evil from her fingertips.

Everything you needed to know about her was communicated in the sideways slant of her '80s bob. It was shaved at the nape of her neck but hung over one eye in the front, so that every time she needed to see, she cocked her head like a shotgun. I'd never seen this haircut before, no one else had it, and its feminine coolness terrified me. I knew to give her a wide, respectful girth. And revere Ashley like a god.

At recess, I kept to myself, sitting on a lone swing. Sometimes Jimmy, the kid with Down syndrome, came and sat down next to me. Jimmy had no idea who I was, but he still liked me. I liked being liked. Plus, when he looked at me I didn't have to stress because Jimmy didn't care about the circles under my eyes or that my pants were gay. He had a rash all over his forehead and couldn't keep his tongue in his mouth. Such a relief. We talked a little, and the unexpected fellowship filled me with a strange sense of purpose. I had not realized the breadth of my martyrdom! God must be so proud of me! *Blessed are the persecuted,* the Bible said. But still, I totally got why Jesus stayed safely invisible, having been previously humiliated and tortured by humans and not planning to repeat the experience anytime soon.

The Bible taught me that when Jesus returned to earth, it would be in a blinding flash of Glory, the sky peeling back, the best pyrotechnics ever seen, and His Chosen—like me—would be lifted up into the air. If only it would happen right now, with all the cool kids standing slack-jawed as they faded into the background fog.

"You fwend?" Jimmy asked. "I you fwend."

It was the most genuine thing anybody had said to me since I arrived in all-white-meat suburbia, but I couldn't answer. I was roused from my humanitarian work by a passing swarm in my peripheral vision. It was a writhing mob of boys who looked to be fighting, until I heard one of them scream, "Ashley!"

I realized, with such a searing and acidic jealousy I could barely breathe, that they were all trying to get to Ashley. To kiss her. To kiss Ashley. She was being mauled by the junior paparazzi. Nine-year-old nerds and jocks alike, all united in a common cause to reject me.

"Get OFF!" Ashley shouted at them, wrenching free and bounding off, her straight, shiny hair going with her. It swung back and forth, back and forth, back and forth, hypnotizing me. I studied the way she ran, wondering what mystical Benetton pheromones emanated from her ultra-Avon pores.

"WAIT UP!" screamed Ellie, chasing after her.

"She might be thirsty!" cried the rest of her ladies-in-waiting.

"Oh my God, we need to check on her!"

Look at that, I marveled. *A posse of devotees.* So familiar. I used to have . . . one of those. That used to be me. Holy moly. My old life. *Stolen* from me.

Why hast thou forsaken me? I prayed silently.

The boys dispersed from their mob and passed through the swing set on their way to the soccer field, laughing and hocking loogies in the dust near my shoes. I leaned to examine the spit splat on my toe.

"Hey, look!" Drew said, nodding at us. "Jimmy has a new girlfriend."

Mortified, I ignored the laughter and stood up, acting like I needed to stretch my legs, or possibly survey the chain-link fence, the vast borders of my kingdom.

"Well," I told Jimmy cheerfully not looking at him, "gotta go."

I wasn't exactly loyal.

Not even when I made my first girlfriend, a kid named Margaret.

Margaret had round glasses and a nonexistent clothes budget like mine, and had committed the cardinal sin against all of Avon: not being thin. Her chances of being chosen for the field hockey team in the sky were slim. But Margaret was different from all the other nice girls in that she was also a real live human being. She could make me laugh, and shared my secret fondness for Jesus, naked Barbies, and simmering with vengeful fantasies.

But it's not like my devotion meant I had the guts to defend her. Like when Ellie waylaid her on the playground one day, flanked by the Johnnies, I decided it was best to do what any decent disciple would do when faced with an imminent crucifixion: Run away. Act casual. Blend into the crowd.

The Johnnies romped and howled around her like a pack of well-groomed, rabid dogs. They'd captured some hapless boy and were trying to corral him toward Margaret.

"We're going to marry the fat kids!" Ellie sang, cocking her hair. The jaws on their alligator shirts were snapping as they laughed, their eyes sharp as fishhooks.

What should I do, I prayed.

When no answer came, I decided to hang back and practice turning my cheeks.

"You have to kiss," one of the boys taunted, pushing the captured boy toward her. Ellie's wicked grin flashed as she presented Margaret with her spelling book, held flat on her upturned palms like a Bible.

"I'm qualified to marry them," she announced to the crowd. "My dad's a minister."

It was hard to believe, but true. Ellie was a real live preacher's daughter. And yet, the Jesus she'd apparently been required to worship was nothing like the fundamentally repressed do-gooder version Margaret and I got stuck with. While ours left explicit warnings about being kind and doing unto others, Ellie's granted free rein to be a ruthless bitch. Lucky for her, in Avon this was the highest calling possible.

"Stop it," the chubby boy growled, trying to elbow his way out of their hands.

From the sidelines, my heart raced, but thankfully the blood in my limbs had slowed to a tarlike crawl, prohibiting me from taking one step toward the eye of the storm. Margaret's pain was too dark and sharp in there, the boys' pleasure too billowy and blinding. They had togetherness, power, and safety. She had only her two arms, folded for protection, her two feet welded to the ground. Surrounded and abandoned, she tucked her head and started to cry.

And thus began my illustrious career of standing by and waiting for the Lord to actually do something.

Because I was a total failure at proper confrontation, I spent a lot of time assuming incorrectly that they'd like us if they only got to know us. We could take back our image. It could happen. We still had Cortney's birthday party.

Cortney was a girl in my class who was cool enough to attract Ashley and Ellie but nice enough to invite, well, us. I knew that if I played my cards right, if I properly networked and gave it all I had, there was a chance I could defibrillate my life.

For weeks, I daydreamed about my epic comeback. Unfettered by the distractions of school, I would amp up my charm to shock-and-awe decibels. I would so tightly control the perfection of my clothes and hair that it would stun-gun them into submission. There would be nothing on me they could possibly make fun of. Nothing. Nada. The only thing sticking out would be my awesomeness.

After school on Friday afternoon, the precarious countdown began.

My brother Kyle, who was six years older and seemed six feet taller, passed by me as I primped in the mirror, a full two hours before the party.

"Are you *still* doing your hair?" He laughed. "Geez, you are vain."

I stopped to consider this.

Puberty had been kind to him. He had arrived in Avon a gorgeous, muscular, wry, aloof specimen of a teenager. Looking at him in the mirror next to me, it was like seeing my physical and intellectual antithesis. He didn't need *Thriller,* he had rock and roll. He didn't need hair gel because he had genetics. Whereas my carefully coordinated cardigan reeked of trying too hard, his shirts didn't match on purpose and his hair remained permanently tousled. He was a Darwinian CEO.

"Ashley is going to be at this party," I explained to him. "This is my big chance."

"Your big chance to be cool, huh?" He smirked. I nodded, liking the way Kyle smiled at me. It made me feel lucky. I watched as he put his clothes by the washing machine, wondering how he'd managed to soak up all the fairy juice from Mom's womb. It was kind of unfair. What about what *my* bone structure had needed?

"This may be my last chance," I told him solemnly.

"Well, good luck," he said.

"Thanks," I said, hoping I'd be one of his kind by night's end. I put on the turtleneck and V-neck sweater that I'd laid out days before—it was an exact replica of the ensemble Ashley had worn the previous Friday. It was totally safe.

Mom dropped me off at the party. With a ladylike but suave air, I entered, ready for the prepubescent Miss Universe. I was quiet and appealing. I said hello to Cortney's mom in the kitchen and presented my submissiveness to the cool girls by averting my eyes. I couldn't believe we were all in the same room together. Hanging out. Eating the same chips. *At your service, m'lady,* said my meticulous outfit and nonthreatening body language. But when I made a sudden movement to exhale, they evacuated, as if sensing TB.

"C'mon," they said to each other. "Let's go in here."

The alphas settled on some boring board game in the living room, possibly because a four-player limit provided just the right amount of hierarchical exclusion, or maybe because their coolness had simply matured beyond stupid things, like having fun. Amazed at their level of self-control and complete lack of imagination, I receded, my faux confidence thinning, into the wallpaper. Maybe they just needed a minute, and then I could play. That was cool. No pressure. All relationships needed a little space. I understood.

I would've prolonged the act, but then Margaret showed up. At first we stood side by side, calm and collected, just keeping it real. But as soon as our eyes locked, I lost my bearings and breathed. Then, I let down my mullet.

I grabbed her by the hand and led her up to Cortney's room where I'd spied a tangled pile of Barbies. Margaret's face lit up, my beloved and willing accomplice to all things stupid.

I picked up a headless doll, my first impulse being of course to find her head and brush her hair. My second being to terrorize the room with her splayed legs.

"Cortney!" I called out, bobbing Barbie in the air. "Come here!"

I wasn't all that friendly with the birthday girl, but I knew her well enough to know she wasn't snobby. I could actually make her laugh in a good way.

Cortney padded up the stairs and popped her head in her room.

"Oh." She laughed shyly. "Aren't those so dumb? I hate them."

"Yeah totally," I echoed, fishing out a Ken doll whose butt had been desecrated with brown marker. "But look! This one pooped itself!"

"Ew, nasty." Cortney giggled.

At one end of her house was popularity, on the other side poop. She seemed slightly torn between the two. I wondered what would happen if Margaret and I could seduce her, win her to the dark side. Wouldn't that make *us* the popular ones? Wouldn't the crew downstairs be *so jealous*?

It seemed like a good Plan B, so to woo her I unleashed a battle cry and chucked Dysentery Ken at Margaret, who screamed and threw it back at me, missing my head but knocking over a radio on the desk behind me. Cortney laughed anyway. Green light.

I lobbed Ken down the hall and over the staircase, where he continued to smile broadly as his rigid body somersaulted, toppling framed portraits in the front hallway. I ran to claim him and Margaret bounded down after me, wielding what looked to be Placidyl Overdose Barbie. For a minute we stood in a standoff, heaving and cackling, the pinwheeling plastic arms of our dolls daring the other to make the first move.

Then Cortney called from upstairs before dropping a few Barbie heads on us, not unlike a mortar attack. Margaret saw her chance and lurched, but I smacked at her with Ken's rock-hard buttocks, then ran toward the closest route of escape, which of course was the living room where the cool girls had clotted.

Margaret ran in after me, screaming something about Ken's tiny weiner.

I was out of control, waving his dirty little neutered crotch bump around like a ninja sword, inexplicably compelled to violate their international airspace. Maybe I thought they'd enjoy Cholera Ken, maybe I thought they'd be open to pointers, maybe I thought they'd be jealous and join in. Maybe I thought God was on my side. But if He was, He hadn't properly equipped me to battle the deadly force of their rolling eyes. Cringing under the weight of their whispering stares I was rendered mute, thinking suddenly about how dumb my hair looked. I touched my cheek, finding a dribble of spit on my chin, proof that my role as Unwanted was somehow predetermined, inescapable. Margaret stood defiantly, waiting for me to continue the game, but I was wavering, shrinking, patting down my hair with my free hand as my laugh trailed off into nervous silence.

"Who invited her?" muttered one of the cool girls. She was tan with dark wavy hair.

Ashley responded with a benevolent little shrug. She didn't have to talk smack. She had minions for that.

"Why are you guys playing with Barbies?" Ellie asked. "Are you like three years old?"

"Oh, my God," said another, "that is so mean." And the group giggled fiercely.

I walked out as if I hadn't heard it, but my rump was steaming from the cattle branding. How could I be so immature, so shortsighted, being myself when *my future was at stake*? Who does that?

It was over now. I was done. It was too late.

Riding home that night, I watched the quaint houses roll by my car window, the antique Colonials and classic Capes. I imagined all the popular mothers standing at their kitchen islands, admiring their popular offspring under their warm, recessed lighting. They'd chat on the phone about their group vaycay at Mt. Killington. The field hockey bags were packed and waiting by the front door. Everything in *their* life was going as planned.

Who invited her? they'd said. I slapped my forehead into my hands, trying to block out the searing playback. If only I was pretty. If only I didn't have such stupid, *stupid* hair.

Every time the light shifted, I could see my silhouette reflected in the car window, each one confirming what they must have seen. I locked in on that signal and fell in sync. At least that way I could understand. At least that way it all made sense. I am ugly, I am ugly, I am *ugly*.

By Monday morning I wasn't quite so depressed. I felt cheeky again, happy to see my dorky friends. At the town fair, my grandma had let me pick out a new red sweatshirt to match my red moon boots. It had LIFE'S A BEACH printed in huge black caps on the front. I didn't know what that meant exactly, and neither did Grandma, but I liked that it seemed ironic. In it, I could skulk past the ski set as a revolutionary.

Look, you snobs, my sweatshirt would say. *Today I've decided that I can never be like you.*

But by Thursday, I'd have on whatever Ashley had on, and by week's end, my solitary thought was, *if only I could, if only I could.*

4 | Church of Christ Barbie

> "I hope to come to you soon, but I am writing these things to you so that, if I delay, you may know how one ought to behave in the household of God."
>
> —1 TIMOTHY 3:14

He was the Englishman in New York yearning to find the meaning of life. She was the all-American girl on a mission to spread the Good News. To God, Mom and Dad must have looked like the hot and cold side of a divine McDLT.

Mom had just graduated with honors from Bible college in Tennessee when she packed her suitcase for the Big Apple. That way she could kill two birds—gettin' into heaven and gettin' outta Dodge—and cast only one dainty little Christian stone.

Dad had just arrived in Manhattan from Great Britain when he glimpsed her up onstage at the '64 World's Fair. She was giving an instructional demonstration for her encapsulated paper company, wearing her encapsulating black skirt and ridiculously pointed sweater. With her magazine-caliber smile and Amazon hips, Mom was the flesh-and-blood version of Dad's first American love, the '57 Chevy. Oh yeah, Jesus knew what He was doing all right. Before long, Dad was on the fast track to baptism and proclaiming the Bible as the one true doctrine.

In the beginning, God created Texas. And this is where Mom and Dad, like all zealous Christians, began their journey. Undaunted, Dad added Southern drawl to his long list of fluent languages and learned to take tea alone. Though they couldn't understand a word he said, his accent encouraged the locals, who believed it was evidence that God's World Domination Tour was in full swing. Soon all of pagan-infested Europe would be swarming into Abilene, begging for a hit of the Good News.

Dad had liked Church of Christ in Texas because it was a big deal. It was a dress-up affair. It was pancake makeup and grand scale and stained glass, cathedrals with polished pews and tall, good-looking preachers who inspired and commanded respect.

But in Connecticut, not so much.

Twenty years later, Dad found himself staring down the barrel of our new church home, or what Dad called a makeshift cattle manger. The New England outposts of the Church of Christ never had enough money to buy a real building. Instead, they prayed every week that God would help us build one. In Connecticut, we drove thirty minutes three times a week to worship in the local community center, a stale, dreary gray room with movable partitions and scuffed plastic tables. It had no glass, and the only thing stained were the sagging panels of fluorescent lighting.

We didn't have real pastors, either, just pastors in training. Young, short and pudgy, they had the sexless, ageless white cheeks and soft hands required of all young Southern Bible college grads. Our slushy gray New England springs and Jewish demographic were a kind of hazing for these budding evangelists. It was believed that an extended mission trip spent hacking at the spiritually infertile soil of the Northeast would make men of them in no time.

When their preaching tour of duty ended, they were given the green light to return to Tennessee, praise Jesus, and a Farewell Fellowship potluck where they'd praise God for our good fortune and tell us how much we'd be blessed by the incoming pastor. Then they'd pack their bags in the middle of the night and flee like fugitives back down into the humid and welcoming pants of the Bible Belt, which gladly loosened a notch as they returned. Down South, the crops for Christ's kingdom were ripe 'n' ready and there were no permits needed to bulldoze. God could have an animated billboard and a sprawling compound with a gleaming white mega-steeple and a massive parking lot that rippled in the heat.

Pastor Pudge, the new reinforcement from our mother church in Dixie, was shorter, happier, and with thicker glasses. Perhaps to help blind him to reality. He was bolstered by a stern-looking wife who left a chill in the front row. Presumably he'd just met her in Bible college, though she looked to be about forty-seven. The joy of knowing the Lord does not always make us more "happy." Behind her pursed mouth, steely eyes and helmet of curls, she was no doubt sizing up her husband as he preached, planning ways to make his haircut more and more like their toddler's. I imagined she had a twisted side, that she drew sad faces on her kitchen serving spoons, each a worse level of spanking, such as medium, hard, and Mr. Extra-Naughty.

Much to Dad's additional chagrin, Connecticut Church of Christers did not dress up for church. They patted down their greasy bed head or wore a ball cap, if you were lucky. In a room fraught with comfy tennis shoes and baggy sweats, Mom, Kate, and I stuck out like sore thumbs in our floral print department store dresses and panty hose. Kyle had on the shoes he wore to junior prom, and Dad of course was trimmed with cuff links and shoe polish, his jet-black hair side parted and sprayed into a surfboard. People watched us pull out of the parking lot with deadpan faces. We knew what they were thinking: *can't take that Acura through the eye of the needle.*

By way of explanation, Dad would remind us, his American kids, that Americans were a bloody sloppy people, and also slovenly, slothy, silty and slitty, and deserving of every *sl-* word in a ranting Englishman's vocabulary.

Dad was the antithesis of slovenly. He'd been raised in Peru by gorgeous, ample-busted *amas* who tidied and cooked and took care of him so Dad's British parents could have more time dedicated to Not Being Sloppy. On top of that, Dad's formative years were spent shuttling back and forth across the Atlantic to English boarding schools where sloppiness was punishable by death. The point being, Dad was hardwired to dress for success. Casual Fridays at work were psychologically painful for him. And as for us ladies, a cross between a Latina-esque June Cleaver and Stewardess Barbie was the unspoken template.

So at the bottom of the stairs before church, he'd perform fashion triage as we descended, ready to pop the loaded question.

"You're going to wear that?" he'd ask as Mom glided down in a pair of orthopedic sandals with ultra-arch support.

"What?"

"Those shoes?"

"Yes. I am. What!"

He was forever trying to get her to warm up to the idea of four-inch heels as casual wear. A frilly push-up bra and a plunging neckline that, Dad insisted, could be worn while one stirred Rice-A-Roni and spot-treating poop stains.

"Sorry, but they're just not comfortable," she told him.

"What's wrong with these?" he asked, digging out the shiny red patent-leather steel-tipped stilettos he'd gotten her for Christmas.

"They pinch my toes."

My dad would look for one of us kids, shaking his head. " 'They pinch my toes.' I knew that was coming."

Mom was queen of comfort. If it was soft and elastic, it didn't matter that the cat had once given birth on it in the garage. Somebody would lob some socks in the trash and she would fish them out, indignant. "Hey! I can still wear those!"

My dad would bring out a Liz Claiborne miniskirt, tags dangling.

"I'll freeze," Mom scolded.

"What about this?" He draped a low-cut black camisole over his arm, now in its fifth year behind dry-cleaning bags. "Man alive, this is what we need!"

"Oh, don't take it out, you'll mess it up."

"Wear it to church."

"Yeah. Right."

"Why not? Of course you can."

"My boobs'll fall out."

"At last!" Then he'd sing his favorite church hymn: "Oh, Why Not Tonight?"

Dad would always lose the fashion war with mom, but Kate and I were open to pointers.

When I presented myself with African-patterned MC Hammer parachute pants and bangs sprayed into a small wedding-cake figurine, he'd ask, in an objective way, "You're going like that, ah?"

"What?" I would say, reading his expression. Could he not appreciate the many modern uses of polyester-rayon blends? The panel of mirrors in the foyer each reflected a small slice of my head. I shadowboxed back and forth to piece together a solid first impression.

"Oh, brother." That was Dad's telltale sound, a verbal British backhand that came down on the first syllable: BROther. Panned.

I'd opt for something more *demure,* which was another of Dad's favorite words, and slip a compact into my Bible, so between hymns I could spot-check to see if the humidity had ruined my chances of being chosen as Abraham's concubine. *We're all beautiful in God's eyes.* Yeah, whatever. That's probably what every slovenly American tourist was telling herself right now, traipsing around Big Ben with a camera and a Big Mac dribbled across her opposing plaids. I may be American, but I sure as hell was not going to be a bloody one.

Kate knew the routine. We shared the same bathroom, mobbed the same wall socket with our own lucky curling irons. We primped ourselves side by side, united in our failure to become Christy Turlington.

"Why are you so ugly?" she asked her face, wielding the brush like a threat. I wondered if I should defend her reflection, out of Christian kindness. But I was too busy thinking the same thing about my own face, and watching the clock.

"We're gonna be late for church!" Dad roared from downstairs. "Get in the car!" Which of course wasn't carrr but *cah.*

Being ten minutes late for church was our family's least favorite activity, and so we did it every week, sometimes more than once.

The good thing was, I could always count on Kate to suddenly crack under all the pressure and make me pee my pants laughing.

At church, we'd start to lose our *demure* right about when Dick, the elderly song leader and also a walking stereotype for Memphis, Tennessee, came up to the podium in his lime green suit to lead us in yet another abysmal tent revival throwback. He'd blow into his tuning harmonica, sing the wrong note, and I'd leer at Kate, who would then tuck her head and rub her eyes to keep from sputtering. Mom would prickle and flash us the first of many warning looks.

Singing became so funny to us because it was supposed to be so serious and so good, and yet it was always so very, very bad. Sometimes this made Dick so upset that he'd make the congregation *sing the dang song twice,* this time *louder* and *with feeling,* as if praising God was supposed to sound like a boys' choir tweaking on meth. Singing was especially critical because there weren't any instruments allowed to cover up our barfy mediocrity. And that was because, along with abstinence from alcohol, dancing, rock and roll, pop culture, shorts, swearing, oh-my-God-ing, tank tops, mixed bathing, and of course premarital anything, Church of Christ was determined also to practice "safe hymns." That is, musical instruments were banned during praise making. Apparently the only thing that pissed Christ off more than an instrument was a beat. Dick was allowed to keep time only by conducting in the air with his right hand. But because of arthritis, Dick could not conduct. He could only stroke his cupped hand up and down in the air, not the least bit self-conscious as he pantomimed the universal sign for jerking off each and every Sunday.

I pretended to cough and Kate gasped into a tissue.

Watch it, Mom's face said. She pressed her finger on my leg, where it left a little white circle.

"What? I'm *blowing my nose*," Kate whispered.

And then Dick tried to make vibrato on a high note and failed, so I dug my fingernails into my arm and stared hard at the floor, desperately trying to block it out, because I knew that once I started, I wouldn't be able to stop.

Finally the song ended and everybody deflated into their seats, pushing their unwelcome perfume around.

"Please turn to song number one twinny-fahve," said Dick. "One. Twinny-fahve."

By the time Dick had finished raping innocent numbers with his accent, and we had finally slogged through five verses about a lamb being quartered and strewn on a bloody cross, I was starving for the Lord's Supper. Which sadly wasn't a supper at all but an unsatisfying tease of a snack, during which the congregation was ironically urged to imagine Jesus's body as a food source.

"This is my flesh," said the Communion leader, as if he was our personal savior. "Take it in remembrance of me."

By the time the shiny aluminum tray with the little paper doily came down my row, my stomach was rolling and growling, starving for some of that delicious, dry, crunchy flesh. However, it was uncouth to fill up on too much Christ cracker. You were to break off only a teensy corner and nibble it into a wad of paste in your mouth, listening to all the crackly pinching and wet chewing in all the rows of hungry, masticating mouths. I closed my eyes and imagined Jesus hanging on the cross. I wanted to be sad, but His legs were roughly the creamy golden shade of a lightly baked pretzel.

"The Roman soldiers whipped and spit upon Him," the leader was saying.

Whipped and spit, my brain echoed as I pinched off a hunk and bowed my head to chew. *Whip and spit, spit and whip.*

I tried to focus.

Imagine getting nailed through the feet. And stabbed through the hands. Ugh, so UNFAIR.

I popped my finger in my mouth to get a piece of remembrance out from behind my back molar.

Then the Men in Charge of the Trays gathered them up and lined up at the back of the room. Then they marched to the front like a squadron of solemn waiters and began to stack the trays. Then they unstacked some other trays and restacked some new ones. As the senseless stacking continued unabated, the red minute hand crawled past the black dashes on the wall clock by the exit sign. Four . . . five . . . six. It was seriously unreal how long sixty seconds truly was.

"Dear Lord," prayed the Communion leader, "please bless us Father, as we drink the fruit of the vine. We're so thankful that, as we drink your son's blood, all of our sins are washed away."

When it came to God's dying son, Christians had a lot of options. You could drink His blood for forgiveness, you could wash your cares in it, you could use it to get stains out of a load of whites, you could even redeem it like a rebate offer and get 100 percent off the price of your sins.

I'd been listening to these catchphrases for so long that I no longer noticed that they didn't make any sense. The only thing that bothered me was that men got to do all the praying. And their prayers were about as inspiring as a sack of turds. *What would I say,* I daydreamed, *if I could lead a prayer?* So many possibilities. It would be like getting a part in the play every week—without even auditioning. But only men got to pray and preach. Men were the heads of the household, the leaders of the church, God's favorites, and even their useless, stinking sack o' turds was more pleasing to God. A woman should never be caught dead flapping her yapper anywhere near the pulpit, unless she savored the thought of an extra-crispy afterlife.

So I waited for him to get to *inJesusnamewepray,* which meant his overpraying was almost complete, thank God, and I was one step closer to sucking down my little cup of Welch's Grape Juice. It was roughly the same color as the deoxygenated blood that must have poured from Christ's puncture wounds. It reminded me of the hymn about splashing in a crimson fountain, only this one was sweeter and much grapier. But it clung to your teeth and left a nasty aroma in everyone's breath.

Then came the trays for the money, and I pulled out my stick of Dentyne like an after-dinner mint, while Mom handed me a dollar to throw in, like a wishing well that would one day magically spit out a new church building.

The prayer leader stood to provide an outline of what his prayer would include, and a reminder that there would be several more prayers before the closing prayer, which cued the beginning of the prayers for the sermon, and then the third prayer before the last five prayers to usher in the final prayer, which would be a brief sum-up of the previous seven prayers, with each prayer lasting about as long as a string of commercials, only with no good show to return to.

"Bow your heads," said the Communion leader.

Sweet Jesus. Church hadn't even started yet.

The only thing it was okay for a kid to play with during Sunday service was, of course, the Bible. I played with its ribbon bookmarker, did pencil rubbings of the fake leather binding, and when things got really dull, even tried to read it. To my surprise, reading it was actually the best idea ever, since nobody bothered to censor the Old Testament. I always thought that God's word was pure. But what child rape scene doesn't sound righteous and pure when peppered with *thy* and *dost*? The dull drone of any given sermon slipped away as I read, growing closer to the darker side of the Lord our Savior.

Men murdered for their foreskins, women stoned for whoredom and their infants cut into fillets, girl children distributed for postbattle deflowering, prostitutes hacked into symbolic pieces and sent via Ye Olde Parcel Post to all thy neighboring tribes, breasts leaping like gazelles and lovers' loins shining like apples.

Then suddenly, God would just materialize and throw you in a half nelson. There was nothing you could do about it except kill whichever people He asked you to, or else your crops, your sheep, and your pecker would wither up and die of some accursed plague.

But—do what He says, and oh, there would be more

knowing and taking and begetting of virgins than you could ever dream of, guaranteed.

God always blessed his favorite men with tawdry delights, like a thousand underaged sex slaves, whom I imagined cavorting nude but for brass nipple covers, strumming crotch lyres, and dribbling cream from their overflowing flagons. Surely, if Noah could have incestuous orgies in his tent, then I, your average suburban child, could long to be groped by a boy's sweaty hand and still escape the wrath of God. I wasn't going to do something stupid, like behead my brother. How idiotically Old Testament.

At the completion of the sermon two hours later, I was transported back to the present day and shuttled with the other young folks to Sunday school for an additional hour of propaganda, followed by forty-five minutes of "fellowship" and finally an hour of putting away folding chairs. By the time we escaped back outside to fresh air, the weekend was gone and evening service was soon to follow. Beyond that, Monday morning and school awaited like an executioner.

"I want you to take this rose, children," our youth group leader said to our Sunday school class. "I want you to pass this rose around, feel free to smell it, touch the petals, do whatever you like with it. Just *enjoy* the rose."

There were six kids, four boys plus me and Kate. It was highly suspicious, being asked to enjoy anything.

By the time the rose had passed through a few sets of fingers it was a bit limp, with a loose petal or two, but still in good shape. The Communion cracker, by comparison, looked far worse after being pressed and pinched by our entire congregation. And it was still holy.

"Now I want to ask you," he said with a gleam in his eye, reaching into a plastic Quik-e-Mart bag and retrieving another rose. His receipt dropped on the floor by his chair. "Which rose would you like me to give you now?"

"Not that one," said one boy, predictably. "It's got everyone's germs on it."

"Exactly," said our Bible teacher, pleased that today's vague metaphor was going so well. *I will lead thee through the lust-ridden manholes of thy adolescence,* he was thinking, *and still make it to the Abdows' buffet by four o'clock.*

"Now, when you pick your mate in life, or maybe even someone you want to go steady with, think about this: Do you want the rose that's been passed around a couple times? Or the fresh, untouched rose?"

Go steady. As if hope chests and knee pants were still possible. In our Bible class manual titled "Pigtails to Wedding Bells," it explained how slow dancing, along with common sense and heavy petting, defiled God's temple.

Heavy petting, I repeated to myself. *Heavy petting. Heavy petting.* Whatever it was, it had to be good. Was it like rubbing your dog's belly, only with more force, and on a boy, while French kissing? Was there light petting? What about straddling, grinding, and kneading?

I summed up the two stems, wishing I could make myself want the poor rose that had been nosed around, but didn't. Nope. I was just another sellout who kinda wanted a fresh rose.

"Can boys be roses too?" I asked aloud.

Our teacher opened his mouth to answer and got stuck, decided to chuckle.

"Sure they can," he said, and I knew right away boys had nothing to worry about. Duh: God liked war, red meat, and intact hymens. He built the entire universe and didn't wear no panties.

"I have another question," I said, not knowing what I was going to say. I was just mad. "Sometimes I . . . *I dance with my stuffed animals.*"

The boys snickered. Our Bible teacher took comfort in the laughter.

"Do what?"

I looked back, enjoying his confusion.

"You're asking me about dancing? I'm, uh . . ."

"She dances with her dolls," said a boy, snorting.

"A *male* stuffed animal," I corrected.

"Are you even old enough to be in this class?" asked one of the boys.

"I just want the rules," I said. The teacher sent an appealing look to his supporters.

"Yeah, but this is really for serious discussion. If you want to talk about teddy bears, I mean, look. Maybe you should be back with the five-year-olds next door."

But I wasn't going to leave it at that. He couldn't suspend me. This wasn't a real class, and this wasn't even his real job. So on Wednesday night I came to Bible class with a pad and pen, a reporter doing an exposé of half-assed Sunday school teachers who couldn't back up their dogma.

I raised my hand and asked about Ken kissing and touching my Marie Osmond Barbie when she had her bathing suit off. They weren't married yet, but they really loved each other, and you know, it was special. What does God think about *that* kind of petting?

Teacher didn't even answer me. He went right on talking about the apostle Paul but told me later I was being rude and immature. I was soundly demoted back to the younger class where I would review the art of shutting up and this-I-knowing about how much Jesus loved me.

I found Mom after adult Bible class was over, still seated in her row of folding chairs, rummaging through her purse. I sat down next to her.

"They're sending me back to the kiddie class."

"I thought they moved you up with the teens," she said, pulling out her checkbook.

"They did," I said.

Mom started writing a check, folding the corner of a paper over the top as a cover sheet. She did that because God doesn't want others to know how much your tithe works out to. That would be tacky, like leaving the price tag on your gift. It was not a gift, anyway, but an *offering*, like a goat you carry on your shoulders to Jerusalem, only with a routing number at the bottom. I caught a flash of several provocative 0s before she folded it in half.

"But I told the teacher," I said, "that I danced. With my stuffed animals."

"Oh, you didn't." She smirked. "Now that's bad."

I could tell she meant the good kind of bad. On the drive home from the community center, I always took my cues from the front seat.

"What'd you think of the sermon?" I'd ask Dad, baiting.

"Don't get me started," he'd growl.

"Honestly," echoed Mom, pushing her hair off her face. "You think they'd come up with something new. Ridiculous."

My eyes gleamed.

Sure, they kept us going through the tiring motions three times a week. But little glimmers of skepticism kept my hope alive. It was clear that no question was too stupid, and no answer very sacred.

That being said, my stupid questions persisted. Reams

of sinful but romantic deeds were still completely unclassifiable. Like, what if you and your Christian boyfriend are the last two people left on Earth after a nuclear war, and no one can marry you, but you have to repopulate Earth? Getting naked and having fornication over and over, whatever that was, would be okay then. Right? And if that was okay, the door swung wide to all kinds of other possibilities. But I couldn't pose sexual scenarios to Mom. And as for these desk clerks running God's bureaucracy? Forget it. They had no imagination whatsoever.

So I explained things to myself like this. God was like the most fair-minded dude in the universe. He would see a problem from every side. He considered not just your actions but also your intentions, your thoughts, He calculated into a divine formula your background, the intensity of your desire, the equation of your entire soul. But none of that really mattered anyway because when He looked at you He would just see love, because God is love, right? And as the embodiment of love, He'd never give girls and boys different, unequal rules because that would render Him unjust and imperfect and unloving. And that was impossible.

At home, I brushed Twirly Curl Barbie's blond hair. She was so tan and hard and unchanging. Like God, she too was perfect. Strange.

I splayed her movable legs and straddled her on the Bionic Man's lap, twisting her articulatable wrist around his head. She had no future groom to please. There was no limit to how many times her petals could be sniffed or her bud ravaged.

Feel me down there, she whispered. *Feel me with your bionic hands.* He wanted to very much, but his appendages didn't bend, so he had to step back and pet her at arm's length like some big grinning dummy. Watching him helped me relax somehow.

Oh, yes, Barbie sighed. *That's right.*

Ken tapped his hand against the hard axis under her skirt, right over her painted-on underwear. Sometimes I wished I were made of plastic too. If I was plastic, I wouldn't have to get ready for evening church because my perfection would be changeless, like my smile, like the shape of my body and my nonexistent soul. As the embodiment of pleasure and beauty, everyone who looked at me would be pleased. There would be no hell, no guilt, no sin, just Ken. Ken and heaven. Lots and lots of heaven.

5 | In a Cabin Down by the River

"Come near so I can touch you . . ."

—GENESIS 27:21

The greatest part about summer Bible camp was that nobody there knew who I really was, or that I was ugly. And even if they did, that knowledge—along with our sin and our lustful thoughts—was supposed to be checked at the gate. It was the perfect place to start fresh and try again to make a new life. Which would last about a week.

At camp we traded in the temptations of telephones and televisions for the old-fashioned pleasures of singing hymns and washing dishes. During arts and crafts, we painted rainbow stripes on plaster crucifixes, and at late-night devotionals, popular kids from other towns stood up to give testimony about how camp had really helped them not hate weird people as much. As I scooted closer to them on the bench, knowing that they were required to act as if they liked me, I grew in the faith that life wasn't about how much they liked me, it was about how much *Jesus* liked me. That was what mattered most. We were not to take any glory for ourselves, but instead deflect it like tinfoil back up to the Almighty, to amplify His holy tan.

Our cabins were divided by gender—girls on one side of the basketball court, boys on the other, so the Men of God could more easily monitor our PDA. The campground itself was in the woods, high up on the banks of the Connecticut River. There were a few breaks in the trees where you could catch a glimpse of the river down in the valley, sparkling in the sun. Far away, cars crossed a drawbridge that spanned in the distance, and flags whipped at the top of the opera house on the opposite shore. But that view was for paying vacationers only and off-limits to Christian campers. Our job was to focus on the view of heaven inside our Bibles, not worldly distractions like natural scenery, unless of course you wanted to get baptized in it.

Our cabin did, however, have a good view of the boys' cabin, and the little swimming pool next to it, where the SWIM AT YOUR OWN RISK sign was hanging crooked on the chain-link fence. But Christians were not so much concerned about drowning as mixed bathing. One look at our soggy, flat, spandex-covered rib cages would propel our brothers in Christ into a lather of sin from which there might possibly be no return.

So as we walked across the basketball court for Girls' Swim Hour, we were careful to wrap our bodies in towels from head to foot. I knew the boys would peek out from their tiny top-bunk windows anyway, straining with sinful anticipation, and it was one of the greatest treats of the day, second only to canteen.

At camp, when we weren't busy denying our flesh, we were praising God in song. Which meant we spent a lot of time singing about sheep. Sheep were God's favorite metaphors, and metaphors were par for the course in one's walk with Jesus, aka Prince of Peace, Wonderful Counselor, and, of course, Lamb of God. Songs about Jesus always alluded to baby sheep: the blood of the lamb, lambs going to slaughter, lost sheep, found sheep, dead but miraculously revived sheep—God loved Him some sheep. It was not unusual at all to sop up some lumpy oatmeal after singing in harmony about bathing in the sweet blood of the lamb.

In the morning, after cleanup duty and chores, there was a series of inspections: military-style cabin inspection, grounds inspection, modest shorts inspection (no more than three fingers above the knee), and inspection for potentially midriff-exposing shirts (reach for the sky, young lady). Then, as a cooldown to the frenzy of repression, we had Bible time, where you found a quiet spot outside to sit and pretend to read God's word.

The picture on the inside of my Bible cover was the happy, laughing Jesus, surrounded by a flock of more lambs. These were still alive. Later they would all be gory carnage, and Jesus would too, but for now they were frolicking in a meadow and having a tragically good time. Maybe they were already dead and in heaven.

Pastor Heath was on the camp staff that year. He was one of the Bible teachers, or maybe the Shorts Master Chief. He was young and looked sort of like John Ritter circa *Three's Company,* which was an unfortunate strike against any aspiring man of God. He did try, in the way that all biblical men do, to be hip.

During morning chapel he'd begin by pinching his eyes shut and praying aloud for the swift and painless death to our independent thought.

"Amen," he'd say, then pause to soak up all the heavenly power. "Now tell me something, you guys. *Dirty Dancing*—really popular movie, right? I want to begin this morning by talking a little bit about that. I was meditating on Scripture last night, when the Lord impressed upon me to remind you that when you girls move your bodies in suggestive ways, do you know how disgusting that is to God? That's why He calls it dirty. Maybe you can't see it or smell it, but you know who can? God can. It smells like dog doo to Him. Imagine showing up at heaven's gates smelling like dog doo!"

Then the boys would laugh at us, and we'd sing and do chores, and the handbell would ring, and we'd repeat the whole thing again. Everyone would sit back down on the outdoor benches, girls on the left, boys on the right. You know, as above, so below. I'd make little designs in the dirt with the toe of my sneaker, and Pastor Heath would pace back and forth with his Bible.

"Boys and girls, we talked this morning about what it means to be dirty, but what does it mean to be clean? I know all you young ladies love to be clean. You sure do take a lot of showers. I walk by your cabins in the morning, and boy I hear that water running overtime. Think about how much time you spend cleaning your bodies, making your body smell nice. But why? That doesn't matter to God. What He cares about is, have you cleaned up your thoughts today?"

My body smells nice, I kept thinking. *My body smells nice, my body, my smell.* I kept picturing naked girls with wet breasts and dark, coiling pubic hair.

Dear God, I prayed, trying to cancel it out with Jesus's face. Jesus was skinny but well proportioned, with middle-parted hippie hair, and he loved to wear a blue afghan over his shoulder.

Please forgive me for thinking that. Amen.

That's all you had to do. It wasn't complicated. Whether the sin was a triple homicide or some suggestive dancing, it was all the same to God so long as you regularly re-reserved your spot in the afterlife by reporting on yourself, and re-repenting.

"Boys and girls," Pastor Heath rambled on, "what is hell like? That's a great question. Well, our wonderful Savior has devised a great plan: to come back at any second and send you straight to hell. And hell is the dirtiest, most filthy place you could ever imagine. A place filled with garbage and dead bodies. Hell is like a garbage dump. A dump that lasts forever.

"So boys and girls, look to your left and look to your right. If your friends dropped dead today, would they go to heaven or to hell? Are they tempted by rock music? Do they tempt others with immodest dress? Do they show contempt for authority?"

A hush went over as the sin-cataloging began.

"Have they been baptized? Revelation 20:10 says those in hell shall be tormented day and night forever and ever. If you don't want that to happen to them, then you've got to bring all your friends to Jesus."

The breeze touched the cold sweat on the back of my neck.

Pastor Heath smiled. "Now raise your hand if you're on God's team!"

Usually, it was hard to get amped about an eternity spent caroling the streets of gold, singing pandering hymns like "Our God Is an Awesome God." Our God was actually an incredibly insecure God, His praise meter always ticking on empty, always needy for worship, a Scooby-Snack to keep His good graces flowing. But compared to having an eternally maggot-infested sunburn, never-ending Sunday school looked pretty good.

"Boys and girls, raise your hand if you are on God's team. Let the Lord hear you!"

"GOD'S TEAM!" we screamed, as if pursued.

During quiet Bible time, Pastor Heath spent a lot of time wandering around with his leather-bound Bible tucked under his tanned arm. He was trolling for an unlucky kid. *Would you like to read together?* It was kind of funny, that poor sucker who had to read the Bible with him, ha-ha. Until I looked up one morning and saw the bottoms of his knee-length camp shorts, waiting.

"Whatcha reading?"

"Oh. Corinthians," I lied.

"One of my favorites. Would you like to read Corinthians together?"

No, I thought but accepted heartily. One must always love to read the Bible with older men, just like in Bible times, when smiling children gathered to lick Jesus's sandals like hordes of hungry kittens.

We meandered to the cement stoop by the girls' cabin, and I sat hip to hip against his hairy arm, sharing a Bible, listening to the whistle of his nostril hairs in my ear.

After what seemed like the longest hour of my life, the fifteen-minute quiet-reading cowbell sounded, he stood up and asked if I would come to his cabin and read the Bible together tomorrow. It wasn't a choice, since this is the kind of thing Jesus would probably ask you to do if He was at Bible camp.

The next morning he was waiting for me, and I followed him with heavy feet, away down the dusty path, away from the other campers, past the mess hall, beyond the camp limits, *good-bye world,* up a lane where you could actually see the river, where cottages for paying vacationers were lined along the overlook. You could hear people being normal, cooking breakfast and watching TV in their little kitchens. It was hot and bright outside, and I climbed up a fleet of blinding white porch steps, feeling icky about this alone time requested by a man of God.

"Would you like a present?" he asked when we were inside.

He handed me a little plastic Bible on a string and promised another for getting through Second Corinthians by the end of the week. He sat down on an upright recliner, Bible opened in his right hand.

"Thanks," I said, wondering where to sit.

"Right here," he said, patting his lap.

It was a horrible thing. His lap, no. Couldn't be. But I strode toward him, like of course! I'll just make myself at home on your thighs, praise Jesus.

Contact with the edge of his hairy knees was mentally painful, so I thought of it like the kitchen counter maybe, a piece of furniture God Himself had designed for fellowship.

"Scoot back, stranger." He smiled, and I kind of laughed, like *oh yeah, sorry.* That's cool. We read Corinthians out of his right hand, love is this, love is that, love is his hairy left arm at ease on the armrest, his wedding band shiny like my dad's but his fingers younger, browner, more alarming.

He's just being nice! I thought. Gross! I tried to think about him as one might think about one's dad, y'know, all fatherly and neutral and Pa-ish. That failed epically, so I mentally retreated to my happy Bible reading place, where the sunlight was dancing and the birds were trilling in the branches, the Old Testament was revealing its friendly R-rated secrets, and there was none of this disturbing crap about love. I narrowed my tunnel vision to the teensy font of his well-highlighted Bible.

I was surviving, three words at a time, when the glorious bell dinged in the distance. I hopped up, salivating for craft time. "Please! I can't be late, I've got to paint Jesus's head!"

"Jesus loves you very much," he told me with a wink. "Do you want to pray?"

Christians could never just end the goddamn thing, whatever it was. There always had to be another ten minutes of prayer tagged onto the second ending of anything. Wringing the listeners of their last drop of hope scored brownie points with the Almighty. Pastor Heath gathered my hands in his and bowed his head.

"Dear Lord. I ask that you help this child grow to be more like you every day, blossoming into a woman of God, knowing you in every way, oh Lord."

I stared at my dirty sneakers trapped between his clean boat shoes and told myself, of course he didn't really, secretly want me and Janet to be his roommates, living downstairs from Mr. Roper. Of course not. The little plastic Bible dug into my palm, slippery with sweat.

"Thank you for this special time of communion, for your special love. Thank you for this beautiful day."

His eyes were shut into little pinches again, searching for more things to thank God for.

"Amen." His eyes opened. "Again tomorrow?"

"Yeah," I said, helping myself to the screen door exit. "Tomorrow."

I blinked in the sunlight, down the steps. Now all I needed was a quarter and a pay phone and a few thugs from Moses's army. Although I knew the angel Gabriel was never freaking going to appear in a dream and help me. I was on call if he did, but in the meantime, for actual real-life help I'd have to phone the earthly hotline of Mom and Dad.

"Hello? Mom?" It was evening, raining hard outside the lone phone booth, which was for emergency use only. Kids didn't normally get to call home from camp, but I'd told my counselor that I was considering being baptized. Excited, she had hugged me and given me all the quarters she had in her portable hope chest.

"Hi!" Dad's voice on the other end of the line was cheery and strong and normal enough to keep the twelve disciples at arm's length. "Is everything okay?"

"Oh! Yeah, great. I think I'm gonna get baptized. And, um, oh yeah. I don't want to read the Bible in Pastor's cabin anymore. It makes me feel weird. Can I just read it alone? Can you call and ask someone if it would be okay?"

Dad: "Do what now?"

God's tender love, I tried to explain, was getting too tender. Yes, I wanted to read Deuteronomy, yes, I wanted to learn all about what God did with the idol worshippers, you know, how He chopped up and basted them in a pomegranate reduction of wrath. I wanted to read all of that, but I just wanted to read about it all alone.

Lucky for me, Dad was my pinch hitter. He'd survived Scottish boarding school, which I imagined was an ice-encrusted prison of stone, where little boys were punished for smiling and made to run barefoot in the snow at dawn. When you've spent your childhood eating blood pudding and getting beaten under your kilt by perverted black-robed vicars, youth pastors who look like lovable bachelors are child's play.

"We'll take care of it," he said. Dad meant it. Sure, God was great, but in order to get anything done He usually required forty thousand prayers and a heavenly host of hot angels singing three-part harmony. But Dad was a business-man. He just needed a telephone.

6 | Our God-Given Talents

"... seek not after your own heart and your own eyes, after which ye use to go a-whoring."

—NUMBERS 15:39

There was a girl at my school who was a perfect pianist. She could master concertos in mere minutes. No song was too difficult. Whenever the choir director needed an accompanist for yet another show tune medley, she was his go-to gal. As long as she had someone next to her on the bench turning the pages, she never made a single mistake. Yet when the audience clapped at the end, she just sat there, hunched and solemn and miserable looking. I never understood how someone so talented wasn't more pleased with herself.

In our family, musical talent, like beauty, was a sex-linked allele and big bro scored the mother lode. Hot and popular and barely seventeen, Kyle was also a virtuoso on the piano who could jam like Billy Joel. He didn't even need sheet music. He didn't even need lessons. He could feel the songs in his hands. From up in my room, I'd hear him settle at the bench downstairs, first a few scales, and then slowly building, until he'd turn loose on the keys and fill the house with music I would later identify as funk. It was a welcome reprieve from Neil Diamond's second volume of *Greatest Hits,* or the Bill Gaither Trio, which tended to get a lot of playtime on the downstairs stereo.

"Why'd you stop?" Mom called out from some corner of the house, whenever Kyle paused for too long. "I was enjoying that!"

Never one to pander for attention, Kyle responded by battering out a round of "Chopsticks." Just for her.

"Booo," Mom called back.

Everybody loved to hear him play. That is, except when he had to read notes. On a piece of sheet music. Then, he became human. Instead of flow and cohesion, there would be halting chords, growling and finally echoing thunder as he'd stomp the pedals.

"WHY?" he shouted at the empty room. "WHY (*thud*) CAN'T (*thud*) I READ (*thud-thud*)?"

I knew why. He was not an accompanist. He was better. He had soul.

I, on the other hand, had the Barbie version of *American Bandstand* to film.

"Hey, pretty lady, wanna dance?" asked dark-haired Ken. I zoomed in with our mammoth-size video camera for a close-up of Skipper's teensy midriff top and hard plastic smile.

"You're kinda hot, Ken," she said. "Okay."

I paused the recording and turned her head to face his.

The dance floor was a plank of Styrofoam suspended between two chairs, so when I poked their feet through, behold, they stood like real people. As I swayed their feet from underneath, they danced together with the subtle grace of human windshield wipers.

The major problem with the choreography was that Barbie's wisp of a torso could not withstand the g-force. As the camera rolled, she fell into a severe back handspring, leaving Ken with only the stump of her pelvis. He seemed not to notice, his unbending arms zombielike around his missing partner.

"Gee, Barbie, you're wicked flexible."

Then, like a wrecking ball into the gentle ambience of Lionel Richie, came Mom's death knell: "Have you PRACTICED!?"

I pressed Stop.

"Everybody take five."

I closed the door on my kick-ass dance club, complete with its make-out loft and Rose Petal Barbie as its half-naked bartender, and dragged myself downstairs to a spare bedroom deemed the "music room." I clicked on the overhead light, which cast a depressingly yellow glow on the carpet. I pulled my antique violin from its velvet-lined case and looked around. Music books everywhere, all stamped with the maddening gibberish of accomplished composers.

Mom had started us on the violin right after we could talk because she heard that Suzuki could stimulate neurological development. But by fifth grade it was clear that Suzuki had not helped me. At all. In fact, my futile donkey braying drove him to loathe me from beyond the grave. But Mom insisted on continuing with the lessons. Our rigorous musical training helped her make peace with her own austere upbringing, where any and all instruments, along with any and all uncovered female legs, and sometimes even breathing, were suspected of highly offending God.

So every day I entered the stringed penitentiary like an inmate and dropped the soap for Vivaldi. I had to use a timer for my suffering, because if I emerged from practicing too soon, my footfalls on the carpet past Mom's room would pop a trip wire in her brain. I'd be almost to the kitchen and—

"I don't know why I'm paying your teachers hundreds of dollars WHEN YOU WON'T EVEN PRACTICE."

"I did practice!" came my predictably shocked response. "What are you talking about? I just did!"

"That was not practicing. That was my money going out the window."

She was right. But sometimes I tried to put up a fight.

"That was fifteen minutes!" I said, rounding up by ten. "Fif! Teen! Minutes!"

Then Dad would walk in from his three-week business trip to war-torn Angola, tired and pissed off and looking for spoiled American children to straighten out.

"Practice the bloody instrument or be done with it," he hollered to whoever was within earshot, spit flying from his lips. "Quit the bloody *styou-pid* lessons already."

It would've been a blessing to all, really. A respectful tribute to Father Suzuki, who rolled over in his grave on permanent press every time I minueted in G. But to Mom, it was candy-assed laziness.

"I agree, let her quit," she said, nodding and shaking her head at the same time, unable to swallow this lump of common sense. She snapped on yellow rubber gloves and began pawing her rag at some dried food on the kitchen counter. She had not suffered through my Sonata for Mating Cats all these years for nothing. Quitting? No. Her daughter would play fourth violin in the Especially Nongifted Chamber Ensemble For Rejects, so help me.

You knew you were under a severe alert when it got to *so help me*. It was the last stop on the train to whup-ass.

"I don't want to quit?" I offered.

"Fine. Practice," Dad said. "That, or so help me, I'm gonna lambaste your backside."

I never knew exactly what a lambaste was, but whenever Dad brought it up I imagined something like a red-hot two-by-four, or perhaps a turkey baster filled with lava, something his child-loathing Victorian British ancestors would've advised. I did not ponder long but hightailed it to the music room, to make hay and let the family suffer through the concerto of my defeat.

I'd done this routine for so long I'd earned default bragging rights.

"I've played violin for seven years," I'd say to friends. They'd suck in their breath.

"Seven years? You must be good!"

The problem was, I completely, totally, and unequivocally sucked. Not just a little bit. But boatloads of pure, unmitigated suck. Seven years, and I still couldn't make any vibrato. I'd tried for years to make my wrist rapidly undulate around the neck of the violin like it was supposed to, like every other girl in the freakin' orchestra could. But I lacked a tendon, or a synapse, or maybe the interest. My end notes always trailed off flat as pancakes, only sharp. Friends would nod and tell me how good I was, their eyes twitching. Judges at Regional crossed themselves as I sawed my way through Bach. I was the great unifier for the line of nervous audition-ers. "Holy shit," they whispered, "we must be good."

I began my daily practice by setting the kitchen timer by the door, like a prison guard. Then I'd start with interpretive freestyle, something like my brother would do. Only mine sounded less like music, more like special effects. Or murdered babies.

"Quit!" barked my mom through her shut door, stuffing the foam earplugs deeper into her brain.

Fifteen minutes to go. Hunched over my violin so that no muscle was unduly taxed, my hair falling in my eyes, I climbed the dull StairMaster into hell known as scales, do re mi fa so, twenty-six times. They were so easy that I could do them while reading about whale blubber, if only I could just slide that *National Geographic* a little closer with my toe. There we go.

Six minutes later, when I was done reading the article and/or practicing scales, I had to man up and face the inverted climax of my day: Pancetta in E or Vibrata Piñata or whatever life-snuffing seventeenth-century masterpiece assigned by Pulowsky, my brilliant Russian teacher.

Pulowsky had defected from the former Soviet Union by rowboat, with nothing but a black turtleneck and a Stradivarius, to seek out the American dream: teaching me. While he imparted the secrets of his brilliant and acclaimed techniques, I stared over his shoulder at the TV.

"What is over there?" he would ask, always smiling, even when strangling me with his eyes.

"Sorry," I'd say.

"Yes, you sorry. Very sorry, ha-ha. Must be good show."

Five years ago he had combed his toupee forward from the back of his neck and it had come to rest in a little wren's nest by his forehead. He wore the same black turtleneck he had defected in, flecked with fifteen years of dandruff. But whenever he played my violin for me, I realized with horror how the concerto was supposed to sound.

The family crept out of their hiding spaces to listen at the open door. Perhaps Mom was paying him all this money so he would occasionally entertain us and thus infuse me with greatness, like essential oils.

"Brilliant," my mom said, clapping as he finished Bach's Gavotte No. 2. "By the way, would you like some pie?"

"Oh," I said, nodding, reaching for my violin. "Oh, I get it now. Thanks."

He handed it back and everyone took cover.

On Thursday nights, it was piano. My three-hundred-pound bipolar piano teacher crawled out of the abyss and slouched toward our subdivision.

Mr. Fretel spent ten minutes dislodging himself from his LeCar. He mounted the front steps, heaved into the wooden chair beside the piano, and spent another ten minutes trying to control his ragged breathing. Then he strained over his belly, grabbed his shin, pulled it up and stuffed his legs into the crossed position. I fidgeted with excitement, trying to keep from staring at him as he slipped a flask out from the chest pocket of his blazer.

"Cheers," he said, tipping it back and dribbling a little pink goo on his beard.

"What's that for?" I asked, scooting closer.

"Antacid," he said. "I have a hole in my stomach. From teaching kids like you all day."

If he was in a good mood, he would torture me only a little.

"Did you hear about the tornado?" he asked as I opened my music book. "It's coming straight for us."

"Huh?" I wheeled around to look out the sunny window, bracing for my greatest fear. He slapped his knee.

"Ha! You are so gullible, my God. Wow. Do you believe everything people tell you?"

But on bad nights, it wasn't just my naivete. It was my lack of technique.

"Terrible," he'd mutter. "Your positioning is the worst I've ever seen. Hold your fingers like this," and his hands arced over the piano keys, floating from note to note like prissy, bloated butterflies. His upper body swayed curtly, like he was feeling the music. But how? How could anyone in his right mind truly feel inspired by a song titled "The Merry Farmer"? Proper technique would require not only proper technique but also apparently an assload of artificial soul.

My musical motto had always been, "If it sounds good, who cares how it looks?" But since I couldn't get the sounds-good part down, I figured Mr. Fretel was probably right. I tried hard to mimic his form, frying every last doughnut in my brain, and still—my wrists collapsed, my knuckles hardened into right angles.

I looked over cautiously at his reddening jowls.

"Didn't I tell you to practice this?" he asked, reaching for his flask. "Do you realize you are wasting my time?"

I felt guilty and semiworthless. He was right. I was wasting his time. But I did practice. That was the thing: six years of piano, practicing five days a week, and I had reached the pinnacle of my ability, plonking "Farmer in the Dell" with two index fingers.

"God," Mr. Fretel sighed. "I'm kidding. Don't look so sad. You're gonna die of brain cancer if you keep stressing out."

"Worrying?" I breathed. "Worrying can't make you get—"

"Brain cancer. Sure it can, kid. You've probably got a tumor the size of a melon in there."

As I palpated the base of my skull for possible malignancies, he played a melody at the top of the keyboard as sloppily as he could, hands flat and sunken.

"Who does this look like?" he asked.

"Me," I said, full of gloom.

"That's right. This is you. Is that what you want to look like?"

"No."

I started the song again, positioning each hand like an octopus with rigor mortis, pinkie aloft. I inhaled for the first chord and went totally blank. Little tumor seeds were blooming all over the anxiety-ridden garden of my gray matter, right this very minute.

Mr. Fretel stared. He bored holes into the sides of my head as he waited. He waited a very long time, but with my hands taking these technically appropriate shapes I could no longer remember what a piano was.

"This is ridiculous," said Mr. Fretel with a sigh.

But what was ridiculous was anyone thinking that I could actually improve. What was ridiculous was the myth that if I practiced hard enough, I would somehow morph into first violin. Or an accompanist. Or Billy Joel. My heart wasn't in any of those things. And when my heart wasn't in something, it didn't matter how well I was taught, or how often. My body simply would not comply.

What my music teachers didn't know was that I did have other talents, other very special talents. I had God-given abilities, abilities far beyond belting out "Woman in Love" in the shower. In fact, they were completely noninstrumental. But, unlike violin or piano, there was no recital for children who filmed graphic Barbie porn and wrote stories about unicorns humping.

My BFF Margaret dialed in for my services. She knew that when it came to fulfilling preteen fantasy, I was a maestro.

"Did you finish the chapter about me and Brian?" Margaret would ask. In real life, Brian was kind of a jerk. But in my capable hands, he was Bruce Wayne.

"Yes," I said, stacking the papers. "Twenty pages of pure lovin'."

"Yes!" she'd say. "Did we . . . ?"

"Everything but," I assured her, "everything but."

It was everything but because I had a block on what the big It was, the actual magical conception part. Tonight, though, maybe I would break through. I was dabbling at another project, the story of Morgan and Macy, two unicorns who'd fallen in love on Noah's Ark. I closed my bedroom door and settled down at my desk in a T-shirt and underwear.

I wrote with colored markers to make up for the absent plotline. There was this delicious tension building, what with all that time in close quarters. Their unicorn love was drawing to some kind of unexpected pinnacle, something that couldn't exactly be included in a classic children's Bible story.

I stared at my bed, wondering.

How did horses do it, anyway?

I really didn't know how people did it either. I knew the penis went in the vagina, but in the name of God how? That was the sketchy part, and field research was not easy in 1986. There were no search engines. There was only a

pamphlet about the mystery of menstruation in my underwear drawer and a vaguely worded romance novel stashed
under my bed. Downstairs, the shelf of aging Encyclopedia
Britannicas could be counted on for disappointingly be-
nign photos of everything. Cross-sectional diagrams of the
human pelvis were not going to cut it. I needed positions; I
needed blunt, eye-popping visuals.

I pulled out paper from a desk drawer. When in doubt,
draft your own. I readied a cover sheet in case Mom burst
in suddenly, you know, with clean laundry or something.
Locking your door was only asking for it. What does an
eleven-year-old have to hide from her family?

I penciled the woman with big round basketball breasts
and dark-colored nipples, and everybody knows about the
triangles of curly hair in the crotch. As for the details of his
member, there was no telling. Just a pale, snaky thing that
hangs. So it goes in the vagina . . . hmm . . . well, however
it goes in. Obviously, she must have to angle around down
under it, but like Santa Claus and the chimney, there was a
degree of voodoo involved. I drew their legs laced together,
their heads at opposite ends of the page. Still didn't reach.
He had bumpy, tumorlike arm muscles, but her breasts were
perfect, and I stared at them until it was almost too much.
Then I picked up the debauchery and folded it until it was
nothing but a tiny cube of paper. I went over to the toy baby
carriage beside my dresser, lifted up the quaint, lacy dolls
and blankets, and considered all the other cubed-up draw-
ings hiding there. This was getting out of hand. I needed to
find another hiding place. I returned to the desk and wedged
the illicit sketch under my pencil mug, for now.

Back to my unicorns.

> *At last we were free on the new earth. Both of us were galloping as fast as we knew how. Our love, the source of energy. Her mane whipped in the breeze and her white figure pulsed at the thunder of her hooves against the earth.*
>
> *Then her shimmering wings unfolded and lifted her up to the sky. With a heave of strength I unfolded mine and joined her.*

A pleasant ache was now growing between my legs. The sounds of the house outside my bedroom faded into the flapping of mighty wings on sweaty skin.

> *The wind caressed us and we glided faster. Then we eased to the ground and I folded my ebony wings tightly to my back. She joined me and I felt uncontrolled. I stretched my neck and brushed her delicate face with mine. The touch of her mane made my heart shiver. As she settled herself on the ground I did the same, easing my body next to hers.*

That's stupid. They weren't going to, what, hug with their legs? But he needed to get his parts touching her parts. Where were her parts exactly? Maybe I could walk downstairs and sort of casually ask Mom, as an afterthought, while I'm grabbing a snack. *Um, so, with horses, like, how do they make love, anyway?*

Make love, are you kidding? Please. I wasn't going to ask her that. We'd had the Talk, but there were still a thousand gaps I'd rather she not fill.

With one last look, I urged her up and then fol-
lowed my soul. We positioned ourselves for the mo-
ment we had waited for much too long. Within a
few moments, all of our dreams were coming true. I
forced myself to work harder to find the utmost crest
of love for this mare. And together we rode it.

I read it over ten times. So sinful, and yet: so much like heaven. All things were possible at the tip of my pen. Churning out page after tawdry page, I didn't need a timer, I needed more time, more paper. Hours didn't drag by, they sailed. My tunnel vision was on the prey, on the love scene to end all love scenes. This was my practice makes perfect, my divinely channeled symphony. This was me feeling the music in my hands. This was my version of soul.

But the fact was, when the masterpiece was done, it didn't look like much. Just a naughty dream scribbled on crumpled medium-ruled paper, hidden underneath a box of appropriate pink stationery in my bottom desk drawer. Nobody got trophies for wishful thinking. Especially not this kind.

I put the paper down and adjusted myself on the seat, found it slippery. Sweet Jesus, I was leaking. I popped up to see if I had somehow peed in my underwear. Was it sweat? Romance-induced sweat? Bizarre. I was ravenous.

Needed Lucky Charms.

I went downstairs and annihilated a few bowls, leaving the marshmallows for last, then went back upstairs to work on the story. I was surprised to find the light on in my bedroom. I turned the corner slowly, horrified to find Mom standing over my desk. My throat seized up, as I tried to act casual, stay calm. But it was too late, my paint-by-numbers porn had already been exposed. She was having a good chuckle, not the least bit appalled, smoothing out the latest intercourse drawing under the light of the desk lamp. I snatched it away.

"Mom, what are you doing! Where did you get that?"

"I was just cleaning up this mess on your desk."

"No!" I said, crumpling up the paper, horrified at the amount of perverted attention I had apparently given the pubic hair. "Don't!!"

I grabbed my strewn novelette in handfuls as the red-flag words jumped off the page: *uncontrolled . . . urged . . . positioned*. I threw it all into the bottom desk drawer and kicked it shut.

"Mom!" I whined.

"Oh, c'mon, lighten up." She had already moved on and was putting clean socks in my drawer. "Have you practiced violin tonight?"

"No."

"Well, it's getting late."

"But *MacGyver*'s on tonight."

"No, no. Don't tell me that now. You had all afternoon to practice."

There was no point in arguing. I was too embarrassed anyway. I went downstairs and set up my music stand in the doorway of the den so I could do scales and still keep tabs on how to blow open a locked tractor trailer with a pair of panty hose.

But tomorrow, I'd do what I'd always done, play fourth violin at Regional, make people yawn at the piano recital, and stand third back from the left at choir. I'd look down enviously at that sight-reading pianist, sitting at the grand piano in her pretty dress, and wonder what it was like to be a child prodigy. To elicit the *oo-aa* from a sea of grown-ups. Compared to me, she was so much better. And yet, at that moment we looked exactly the same, frowning through the applause, wishing we were somewhere else.

7 | Reflections of a Mirror Addict

"Can a virgin forget her ornaments,
or a bride her attire?"

—JEREMIAH 2:32

At Avon Middle School, my oversize self-hatred
bloomed right on schedule with my undersize
breasts.

I figured what I needed was a perm. *Yes,* my undeveloped
mind plotted, *a perm—then, THEN they'll finally love you.*

However, the beauty tech at Sheddin' Sam's had other
ideas, like tipping the scale in favor of my preteen suicide.

After washing out the putrid chemicals and blow-drying
my coiling mullet into a hair helmet, she spun the chair
around and I wept openly.

Where is your sense of duty? my wet eyes implored.
I looked exactly like the geek from *Sixteen Candles.* No,
worse, I was my grandma. I looked like my grandma. Only
Grandma was prettier than me.

At home I stuck my head under the bath faucet to try to
start over.

But with bodies, you couldn't just start over. You pretty

much had to work with what you were given. And there was nothing about mine that was obeying the predetermined, primordial Christie Brinkley mold I had prepared for it. It was pudgy and skinny and huge all at once, all in the wrong places. My face was the antithesis of symmetry, my midsection the sworn enemy of svelte.

Svelte was a peculiar but all-important word that I gleaned from Dad's vocabulary. Everything on a svelte woman was miniature, tightly contained, and doll-like, particularly her butt and her waist. She looked naturally made of plastic. And it never mattered what she wore, you could tell she had nothing to hide under her clothes. Except maybe that stamp on her crotch that said MADE IN CHINA.

Sveltes were everywhere, and my dad always seemed to notice them first. At a family restaurant one night, he eyed our petite waitress and nudged Kyle in the booth.

"What do you think?" Dad asked him. "Huh? Very svelte?"

There it was again. Annoyed, I wiggled up next to Kate in the booth and pinched a hunk of her padded bra.

"Very svelte," I said.

She locked my wrist and grabbed the belly hanging over my pants. "No, that's a hunk of svelte."

It was such a relief to have Kate. At least we could be huge and wrong and mediocre together.

"Stop," said Mom, eyeing the elderly couple in the booth behind us.

"Why don't you ask her out?" Dad poked an elbow at Kyle, trying to kid him to life. "Huh? Huh?"

"No! She's too flat chested," Kate whispered.

"She wasn't flat, was she?" said Dad, looking concerned.

"That's every pirate's dream," Kate said. "A sunken chest."

"Is that what you tell yourself these days?" asked Kyle.

Mom: "Hurry up and order."

"I'd say seventeen. And cute," Dad went on, sizing her up. "What's to stop you from asking her what high school she goes to, at the very least?"

Kyle said nothing.

I didn't know why this was an issue. All the girls loved my brother. His last girlfriend was Miss Teen Connecticut, for God's sake. He went to prom with a girl you could fit in your glove compartment. Big bro was a waif magnet, and Dad a lover of svelte, surrounded by a booth of genetic Amazons.

"He's ashamed of his family," I explained, spraying crackers out of my mouth as I chewed. My white plastic earrings were as big as tire irons and banged against my jaw.

"She's got a nice figure," Dad went on. "Very svelte."

"Dad," said Kyle, trying to summon the words. "Dad . . ."

"Do you hear what your husband is saying?" I interrupted, looking at Mom over her menu. I felt she should pay closer attention. How could a woman with so much junk in her trunk be oblivious of this ongoing worship of the ninety-pound woman?

"What?" she said. "It doesn't bother me."

She always said that so convincingly, but I didn't buy it.

"I'm confident in myself," she added, to further throw me off the trail.

Confident? But according to every movie I'd ever rented and every actress Dad had ever loved, a woman needed to be under ten percent body fat. Which is why Kate and I had started eating only fat-free packaged foods. We carried fat-free dressing in our purses and ate cartons upon cartons of noncaloric frozen dietary desserts. According to *Young Miss* magazine, there was pure absolution right on the label: *fat grams . . . 0*. While I tore through three entire fat-free chocolate loaf cakes in mere minutes, licking the crumbs off of my plate and scraping the cardboard packaging with my front teeth, Mom calmly helped herself to a bowl of extra-creamy Häagen-Dazs.

Mom was at peace with her body. Which shocked me, because puberty was beginning to reveal that I had a carbon copy of hers, especially the inherited lack of a waistline. Pants placed properly on our bodies—with comfort in mind—had but one name: Urkel. I tugged all day long at elastic waistbands, coaxing pants back down over my pelvis while hunks of my upper butt spilled over the sides, creating another amorphous thing to hide. Meanwhile Mom's shorts rested at ease near her breasts, and she ambulated in what seemed like a cloud of pure comfort.

I sighed, watching Sveltie the waitress bend to pour coffee, amazed at how her clothes lined up effortlessly with her torso.

"She's probably eaten like three grams of fat this entire week," I pouted.

"I like her hair," said Dad. "She's fluffed herself up."

Dad called it fluffing yourself up, as if all a woman needed to do was take a shower and point a blow dryer at her face, and voilà! Fluff, glorious fluff. The hills are alive with mounds of fluff.

But fluff, when deployed upon my short, permed mullet looked more like puff. Less Debbie Reynolds and more

Grandmas Gone Wild. It was more of a cry for help than a hairstyle.

Nevertheless, I got up at the crack of dawn every day to follow my own rigid regime of hair fluffing. On the day of the class photo, fluff had to be ironclad. There was a tight-rope of chance to walk between each stage of washing, conditioning, hair drying, and volumizing, or else the fluffing could fall, like a cake.

At eight twenty-five a.m. Mom was out in the car, laying on the horn, while I begged the last nip of hair to please, please, for the love of God, fluff! *Fluff, damn you!*

In line for class pictures, I waited my turn and practiced my nonsmile again. I was determined this year I would sneer like a model. No more goofy, crooked smiles on the mantel for me. No way. Not this year.

"Smile," said the cameraman of the masses, waiting.

My face was unmoved.

"Smile for me." I looked deep into the camera, whispering with my eyes: *No smiling.*

I had just watched another National Geographic special, titled *The Science of Beauty.* I tried to explain my cache of new factoids to the poor idiot photographer.

"Did you know if you show a baby the picture of a supermodel," I said, "the pleasure centers in its brain light up like a Christmas tree?"

The photographer stared into his lens.

"It's called symmetry!" I laughed nervously. "Isn't that neat? It means even if the model eats the baby as it crawls toward her, the baby will die happy because her face is, like, so frigging SYMMETRICAL."

"Honey," he said, "I've got a long line, could you please . . . ?"

"See, I'm naturally asymmetrical," I went on. "When I'm happy, I get crooked. I mean, I don't know what happens, one side of my face just, like, seizes up. Last year? I tried to think happy thoughts and just sort of exude joy, so that my inner beauty would shine through . . . like this?"

I flexed last year's smile and there was a blinding flash.

"But wait . . ." I said. "I was trying to explain . . . it didn't work."

"Next."

Weeks later, a popular girl on the field hockey team delivered the photos to my homeroom, peeking at each one before she handed it over.

"Wow," she quipped to me, "nice hair."

Hard to take it all in at first, but my huge, overfluffed bangs were like a massive brown squirrel that had curled up near my eyes and died. The swirling blue backdrop loomed like a pastel nightmare over my squinting eyes and drooping lip. It was like I'd just come to after being slapped upside my head with the ugly stick. It was a campy version of *The Scream*.

I took the proofs into a stall to vomit on them but had no luck with my stubborn gag reflex. I knew what guys did—they flipped through the yearbook like it was the *SI* swimsuit issue: *smoking hot on page 12*, they'd say. *Nice tits page 27.* Then, for me: *Dude—this chick needs a BAG over her head, page 43.*

I got in the car and handed the photos to Mom.

"Adorable," she said.

I kicked off my pointy flats and discovered my feet were now shaped like pointy flats.

"I don't want to be adorable," I said. "I'm so hideous!"

My mom dropped the pictures in her lap, peeved. "Honestly, why would you say something like that?"

"Because it's the truth. Look." I pulled out the dizzying stream of wallets, a million horrific little heads, all of them mine.

"I can't believe I spent all that money on braces and you won't even show your teeth," she said, holding up a monstrous 8 x 10. "What a waste."

She put the car in Drive and shook her head.

"Be glad you have teeth. What if you were in a wheelchair? What about people who have burns all over their faces, and arms missing?"

I rolled my eyes, which meant, duh, I practically already had no face and two stumps. There was nothing to feel lucky about.

If I looked like the varsity field hockey captain, I knew, then I'd have something to be thankful for. If I had a swarm of jocks begging to check me for ticks, I'd get grateful in a damn sure hurry.

"I'm ugly," I announced, crying.

"You look cute!" she said, a trace of panic in her voice. "Honestly, I don't know why you make such a big deal!"

But that's what middle school was all about. Everything was a big deal, and the biggest deal of all was where you sat at lunch.

I sat at a table with Mallory, Lisa, and Margaret, and a new girl named Joann. A few feet to the left, invisible barbed wire marked off our dork demographic. I knew why Margaret and Lisa and I were here, but Joann—why Joann? She had really good clothes and two BMWs in her three-car garage at home. She'd even named them, like Bev and

Bernie Beamer or something. She had everything you'd need to be popular in Avon but possessed some nameless quality that had cost her the winning ticket. Maybe she shrank a little when people looked at her. Maybe it was because she'd never learned how to be an asshole. Whatever it was, the gods of Avon had deemed her defective, so she sat with us.

On the other side of the razor wire were tables packed with girls trying to lay claim to Ashley and Ellie and the twins, Christy and Carrie. A few popular guys sat with them, the laces in their oversize Nikes dragging on the floor behind them like peacock feathers. Occasionally one of them would reel an arm back and pelt our table with hard candies. Then they'd hunker down and laugh.

"Oh, my God," said Joann, ducking a butterscotch. "Who did that?"

I knew exactly who did it. I was aware of every movement at every table in every quadrant at any given moment. But the best defense was to not notice the offense, even if it hit you in the head. Plus, I hated confrontation. It was easier to burn with unrequited hatred. I ate my chicken patty and watched them, taking mental field notes about life in the green zone. What was it like to be so safe? What did they talk about? I couldn't hear a single word, but I knew. I could taste on my tongue every little inside joke they whispered into the shiny shanks of their long hair. It was not unlike the residue of my reconstituted poultry by-product.

Ten minutes before the bell, these girls moved as one, like a flock of birds at the watering hole, panicked by an unseen cue.

"Wait for me, Ashley!" the girls called, struggling to stay together.

"Ellie! Wait!"

"Everybody WAIT!"

And then, scattered trash and silence. The barometric pressure dropped a degree, the atmosphere stabilizing.

"Hel-*lo*," Joann sang next to me. "You're not even listening to me."

"What?" I tuned back in. "I'm just spaced out today."

I left lunch with Joann but veered off toward the bathroom. I had to. In the hallway, the slightest glance my way felt like it burned. I could hear people whispering about me, about my hair or my belt or my shoes, picking me apart like vultures. Their opinions amplified into a quiet roar in my head that stilled only in the heart of the bathroom, where I could hide, where I could reupholster my face and reshape the collapsing architecture of my hair. Without constant maintenance and monitoring, punishment and control, how could I possibly handle fifth period? Or sixth? Or seventh? Or the rest of my life?

I looked back at Joann and said nothing.

She sighed.

"You just went in there five minutes ago! Come on, you look fine."

You look fine. Please. If I looked fine, people would be killing themselves over me. And, I wouldn't have to glue my pretty back together with hairspray every seventy-three seconds.

"Just gotta pee real quick," I lied.

"Yeah, right," said Joann, walking off.

Why couldn't I just be normal, eat lunch, go to class, smile and giggle, rinse and repeat. My life had been like that once. People had looked right at me, right dead in my face, and I'd been able to look right back without feeling terrified. How had I done that? I couldn't remember anymore. My face had changed so much. It was changing every second. I had to control its complete unraveling, or else . . . what? I'd go up in flames. I'd go extinct. And forever remain the butt of every inside joke.

I pushed open the heavy swinging door and went in, the air muggy with the dueling odors of shit and soap. There were girls standing by the sink, so I sauntered into a stall and closed the door. I stood inside, listening to them washing their hands and ripping paper towels. I flushed once or twice to prove that I was attending to bodily functions. But I was really just standing there.

When the last person left and the bathroom was finally quiet, I emerged and went to work like a spy, setting out my arsenal of tools: lipsticks, concealer, travel-size curling iron, and the big gun, a can of Mega Hold. Ironic, since my goal was to give the impression that I didn't use hair spray. My goal was to look like Ashley, like I just rolled out of bed in the morning and tucked it behind my ear and—poof— natural beauty. The cover of *Seventeen,* the mannequin at the mall with only whites for eyes, hard and permanently flawless and worthy of pedestals and spotlights. But I had no natural beauty, so I squared up with the mirror and readied myself for the wave of disgust. Then I held my breath, tweaked and realigned, sprayed and prayed, doing my best to zero in on the unfixable problem.

I prayed a lot about my mirror issue. I felt a little better when I was done praying, but nothing much changed. After all, it wasn't God's fault. He was on my side but it wasn't like He could step in and give me a new head. God was good for healing sicknesses, for protecting you from enemies and bringing Joy to the World. Understandably, sorting out why I was so hideous was way below His pay grade.

Still it was kind of ironic how God, who was supposed to see only our hearts, ironically chose only the comeliest maidens for the Bible's best supporting roles. You couldn't just be virtuous. You had to have towering breasts, alabaster skin, and a temple so bodacious that all of Israel would want to beget with you.

A random girl walked into the bathroom, startling my trance.

"You," she marveled, giving my array of weapons the once-over, "are always in here."

How did she know? I tried so hard to stay so invisible, to be so careful, and still. People knew I was always in here. Ugh. I scraped everything back into my book bag and pretended that I was done—even though I had barely begun. I pretended to be looking for something. *Where is that, um, folder for art?* Yeah, I need that folder. Hmm, must be in here somewhere. I could feel her looking at me, waiting. She smelled my fear.

"You are *always in here*," she said again. What made her think that pointing out my behavior would make me do it less? Yes, I was always going to be in here looking at myself, but that didn't mean she got to watch me do it. I bent over to rummage deeper into my book bag, up to my neck in my Trapper Keeper, looking for a hole to China.

By the time she gave up and left I was thirteen minutes late for Spanish, and my bangs were tall enough to receive messages from space. I hurried down the empty hall and slipped into the back of the classroom, keeping my head as low as possible. The teacher marked me late. But I waited twenty minutes, got a bathroom pass, and tried it all over again.

Maybe it was the shape of my head. The shape of my head went with nothing. It wasn't a diamond or a pear or an oval like the head chart in *Seventeen*. It was a sprouting potato.

As if on cue, two boys near my locker started examining me.

"Holy shit," one of them said to his friend. "Look, dude. Look at her from the side."

"Oh, yeah, weird. Pop-out eyes."

"Gross."

I stood still and said nothing, waiting to see what else they would find. Then I raced to the janitor's closet to examine my profile.

Oh, no. I completely overlooked that whole side of my eyes. They bulge? They bulge!

In the next class I snagged the seat against the farthest wall and hid behind my hand. How long, I wondered, had people been recoiling at my *bulging eyeballs*? There was no telling. How was I going to deploy my camouflage while still seeming casual? Maybe I could just constantly massage my temples, or rub my head, while using the rest of my hand as a veil, so no one would see my face.

That worked for a little while. Until I was in gym, running sprints.

"What's wrong with you?" girls asked through the tunnel of my cupped hands.

"Oh," I said, covering my face. "I have a headache."

Gym was the biggest low of the day. The hair destruction caused by bodily movement was unreal and almost always irreversible.

In the crowded locker room, I reluctantly brought out my Mega Hold, the holy mist. It was so stinky that in close quarters the other girls clawed at their throats, dropping and rolling in the toxic cloud. It was probably tested on animals, sprayed in the clamped eyes of defenseless bunnies, then scented with the pulped pituitary juices of their dead bodies. But I had no choice; it was the only hair goo that came in a four-ounce size and could fit discreetly in my book bag. Ignoring the comments, I held my bangs just the way I wanted them to stay forever and ever, amen, and crop-dusted my shoulders.

I left the locker room with my head down as low as it could possibly get on my neck, since I couldn't shield my pop-out eyes while also lugging my backpack, my portable makeup and hair studio, and my plastic sack for my gym clothes, which was weathered and sporting holes and needed be to supported from the bottom. That night I would painstakingly reinforce it with Scotch tape, since it was the only proof that my family had once purchased something from the Gap. Last year.

I veered off into the empty Home Ec room to pull out my compact, but it was too dark to see. So I held it out in front of me as I walked down the hall, pretending there was something in my eye, so I could monitor the effects of changing light and humidity. Oh, my God, I was even uglier than I was ten minutes earlier. I was hemorrhaging ugly.

In math, the teacher marked me late and told me this was the fifth time and it was going to cost me a detention. Marinating in concealed panic, I took my seat in the middle row, my back inches from desks occupied by the Twins.

To my immediate right sat a boy who'd scraped I LOVE CHRISTY on his forearm in what looked like his own blood. That same boy had hocked a loogie in my hair last fall. I had come home crying about it, and Kyle had said, "Trust me, he probably likes you."

"And the boy who taped KICK ME to my back and called me shit for brains?" I had asked him.

"Yeah, he probably likes you too."

"At what point do they tattoo your name in their skin with a paper clip?"

"That's just stupid."

"Do they secretly hate the girls they pretend to like?"

Cornered, Kyle had turned to strategy. "Okay, next time he says something, ask him if he thinks it's cool to pick on a girl."

I agreed, but what I really needed was for Kyle to accompany me to every single class, wearing his varsity basketball jersey. That would shut them up.

Immediately after I took my seat in math class I realized with horror that I could still smell the deadly Mega Hold. If only I'd taken one more lap up and down the hallway to let it evaporate. The room was so hot and humid that the odor could not be missed, it was like stale, sweet formaldehyde. The twin hyenas behind me sniffed the air.

"What is that?"

"Oh, my God, that totally reeks."

Dry, dry, dry, I prayed. *Please God, let it dry.*

"Hey," said the I LOVE CHRISTY boy. He was talking to me. I stared deeply at problem 122 on page 43. He poked my shoulder with his pen. I turned, prickling, to see that he had pulled his shirt over his nose.

"Is that like perfume? Or did you forget to wipe your ass?"

A twin hushed him with a little slap on his shoulder. More of a caress, really. Then she and her sister retreated behind their identical folders for an identical laugh.

"Oh, my God, Jeremy! You are so mean!" They giggled.

I looked away in order to turn the other goddamn cheek. Plus, I didn't want to offend him with my ginormous pop-out eyes.

"Why do you always smell bad?" he asked.

Ah, this must be codespeak for *can we go out this Friday?*

"Why do you think it's cool to pick on a girl?" I blurted, then took cover by looking the other way.

He said nothing. Maybe he was surprised. Maybe he was unaware that I had a speaking voice and the ability to hear. But he went silent.

At home, I sat in the kitchen souping up my second bowl of 100 percent fat-free Crispix. In the other room, Kate was sitting on the couch channel surfing. A National Geographic special was on, showing a variety of male creatures preening their rainbow feathers and dancing for show, locking their massive horns and bearing claws and goring themselves to bloody messes just to impress one homely brown female. She wasn't pretty. Just a plain ugly bird, like me.

I stopped eating and stared. It was so different for humans. All males had to do was learn to belch the alphabet, skateboard, and play video games. Oh, yeah, and keep girls like me in their place. When it came to winning love, the real battle belonged to us females.

Kate clicked on one of the networks just in time to hear the ominous thunder roll of a tympani as two spotlights glistened on a stage.

"It's on tonight?" she yelled, surprised. "What time is it?"

I drew closer.

"It's on tonight!" I echoed.

It was. The pied piper of young girls, the fascist wood chipper of their impressionable hearts. The Miss America pageant had just started.

Tagged with numbers, parading their lean skirt-steak

flanks in the spotlight, their smiles fierce and their hair halos luminous. Worthy of spotlights and sequins and crowns, they carried the survival of the human species on their dimple-free hindquarters. By comparison, my body was clearly a factory second. I looked down at my bowl, but the digestion of my cereal had ground to a halt.

"They rub Preparation H all over their butts," Kate told me excitedly, her eyes glued to the screen. "It hides the cellulite. Tightens the skin."

I knew what she meant. We couldn't afford to like this too much, the harbinger of what was coming in our lives. Happy endings were slipping farther and farther out of our trajectory.

"Where's Miss Connecticut?" I asked, trying to be hopeful.

"She's the one in the blue," Kate said, and I squinted. Yeah, okay, she was . . . okay. Crap. She wouldn't survive the first cut. She wasn't Barbie enough. She didn't rape your eyes with her spastic perfection and her fiberglass buttocks like Miss Texas did.

I set my bowl in the dishwasher and paused one more time in the doorway to watch a Maybelline commercial. The model kicked the surf with her long beige legs, laughing in slow motion as one might when in the throes of self-love. The hunk in the linen shirt caressed her teensy waist, mesmerized by her weightless body.

Maybe it's Maybelline!

"Maybe it's hemorrhoid cream," I called back to Kate, as consolation. "All over her face."

"Yeah," she said. "That's funny."

Neither one of us laughed.

• • •

Halloween Day at school was my get-out-of-jail-free card. It was the one day where looking weird was condoned, and I could finally embrace some negative attention. I planned my costume for weeks. Head on a platter maybe, with zombie-like makeup? Nah. Half-man, half-woman? Human electric socket? After much deliberation, I decided to tone it down a bit, maybe something more sardonic and obscure, like candidate for president.

I laid it out on my bed piece by homemade piece: man's suit jacket and tie, American flag do-rag and boxers, red Converse high-tops, and a VOTE FOR ME! button on the lapel. Yes! It was a random ensemble, but I imagined the entire school would be so impressed by my double entendre, and so glad that the bandanna covering my forehead would prevent my bangs from taking over the town. I was so excited. I was so scared.

Mom snapped my photo on the front steps and asked me what I thought was on voters' minds.

"Change," I said, and jingled the coins in my suit pocket.

Then I walked into the fluorescent light of the school foyer and froze. What voters had on their minds definitely wasn't coming to school dressed like an idiot. No one else was doing Halloween. Duh, we were too old for that. And my costume wasn't funny ha-ha. It was funny weird.

"What is she wearing?" Passersby asked themselves. "What the hell?"

Just be yourself, whispered Jesus.

Oh, crucify me.

A random girl by my locker covered me with a once-over that was like being smeared with shit.

"O-kay," she sang.

"Halloween," I explained with a friendly laugh.

"You need serious help."

"Thanks."

Why did I always thank people? I meant it to sound sarcastic, but it was always too quiet to be heard.

Mr. Tanner understood me, though, bless his delectable soul. Mr. Tanner was my English teacher and lone beacon of hotness and hope. Late thirties, twinkly blue eyes and sandy hair, sexy, funny, and fodder for my naughtiest journals. I had written several stories in which we'd made out passionately, and he'd left his wife and newborn twins so we could gyrate together on every beach in the Northern Hemisphere. He always wore this adorable little bow tie and sometimes even juggled copies of eighteenth-century classic novels. His motto was, "Be a dork," and ironically, the cool girls couldn't get enough of him. They gathered like groupies around his desk before class, fawning.

"You *are* a dork," they'd gush, salivating. "Total nerd."

For Halloween, Mr. Tanner was totally decked out in clown gear. Of course he was. Truly stupid looking. He was so brave.

"Hey, Mr. Tanner!" I said grinning, throwing down my backpack. "Whadya think? Get it?"

I spun around once in my boxer shorts, flaring my suit jacket, and he studied me, resting his chin in his hand.

"Okay, wait," he said.

"Aw, please say you get it."

" 'Vote for Me.' Ha. Very original, like, what, flasher for president?"

"Sort of," I said, twisting, wishing I had thought of something that clever.

He turned around in his clown shoes. "What about me, too subtle?"

"No, you're perfect." Indeed he was. Dreamy. But so tragically married. Ugh.

"Geek power." He grinned, and I grinned back, completely blank and stuttering in the presence of his red foam nose. I looked at the shape of his hands, masculine and sturdy, and melted.

Then some popular girls entered and swallowed him whole.

"Oh, my God, Mr. Tanner!" they screamed. "Nice outfit!"

"Hilarious!"

"So dumb! But I love it."

As I watched them, I turned invisible again. Little pieces of their superior hair, their more attractive fingernails, their tan ankles and unabated group happiness—it canceled me out.

A terrifying jock I'd never dared talk to in my entire life dropped his book bag near my desk and summed me up. Out of the corner of my eye I could see him shaking his head.

"Oh, my God," he said, moving in for the kill. "*Why* do you have to sit near me. Why?"

I struck my default I-can't-hear-you pose.

"Nice zit," he said. "Why are you dressed like a homeless man?"

"Go away," I muttered, my interim comeback until I could spend several years preparing a proper one that I would deliver boldly, but only to the mirror.

"Ashley, look," he called out to no one, still staring at me. "Look, it's your twin. Not."

I wondered what he meant. Did I act like a copycat, even in costume? I grew sullen, the edge of my festive bandanna burning my skin.

"You think you're so hot, don't you?" he persisted.

Oh, no.

I pulled out my books, placed them on my desk as if they mattered, as if I cared about homework, or school, or anything besides escaping. A hush fell over the class as Mr. Tanner began talking, but I could still hear the boy next to me, whispering to his buddy. A spitball or two crossed my desk. One hit my shoulder and stuck, which meant I had to brush it off, which meant acknowledging that it was happening. I flicked it off and swallowed hard, staring straight ahead at pages with words that made no sense.

Dear God, I prayed. *Please.*

I waited for an answer, but could hear only my own thoughts speaking in a movie voice.

They must fulfill prophecy.

I took one glance at the boys and they looked away, laughing quietly.

Why was I praying? I needed earthly help.

When the bell rang, I gathered my things and hovered around Mr. Tanner's desk again, waiting for the class to disperse. When the room was empty, he smiled up at me, gathering his papers.

"President-Elect?" he asked. "What can I do for you?"

"Um," I mumbled, "I'm kinda having a problem."

"Oh, yeah?" He paused and did a double take. "What's going on?"

He had taken off his clown nose, and his hair was slightly pressed down where the wig had been. There were tiny smile lines in the corners of his eyes. He was so tall and experienced and happy, so achingly hot. The exact opposite of everything I was.

"I don't know, it's a couple boys, I guess."

I watched the surprise on his face and wondered. How could he have missed the spitballs in my hair?

C'mon, my eyes pleaded. *Geek power? Remember?*

"I'm sorry I never saw that," said Mr. Tanner, and I knew he meant it. "But sometimes guys act like jerks . . . when they like you."

"Yeah," I managed, and choked on my escaping air, trying to turn it into a polite laugh. *Maybe,* I thought with growing horror, *maybe you've never actually been a dork.* "Yeah, but trust me, I really don't think they like me."

"Let me talk to them," he said. "Hang in there, kiddo."

I looked right at him and for a moment felt certain that he saw me and not my face, and that he cared. I nodded automatically, suddenly not even thinking about how I looked.

Still, there was not much feeling of relief in getting my hot teacher to fight my battles for me. There was even less when the boys shuffled over to me the next day in class, flinging folded-up apologies at my desk, eyes averted, mumbling *sorry.*

I opened their letters in the stairwell after lunch, filled with dread, trying to decipher the boy scrawl.

I'm not sure what I did, one read. *I really didn't do anything. But whatever it was, I'll try not to do it again I guess.*

Paper wadded up as spitballs or wadded into apologies. I wasn't sure which was worse. Probably this.

8 | Lunch on the Shitter
(One Teen's Walk with Christ)

"God is coming . . . He is coming to save you."

—ISAIAH 35:4

I don't remember why Cortney started hanging out with me during our freshman year. She was such a beautiful girl, gentle, creative, with lots of cool friends. It didn't really make any sense, so I just assumed that Jesus had sent her to me to be saved.

As we sat in her room, redecorating—dipping sponges into paint and pressing them into half-moons on her wall—I daydreamed about walking the scary corridors of Avon High School with her by my side, keeping me safe from harm. Such a good look for me!

Thanks to her popular older brothers, whom she hated, Cortney was an insider to any and all venues of hot sex and hard drugs on a rich-town Saturday night. Stuff people like me were born to judge while eating popcorn, hanging on every word. She'd been doing bad things with cool people, and yet here she was with me! I was over the frickin' moon! But only because I wasn't allowed to frickin' swear.

On the other side of her messy shag-carpeted house, I could hear one of her brothers blasting John Cougar Mellencamp.

"I hate him," Cortney muttered, wiping her sponge on the edge of an aluminum paint tray. "I fucking hate him."

That was shocking: hating one's brothers rather than standing in awe of them. This is what happens, I realized, when Jesus was not around to properly affix your thoughts. Oh wait. Maybe she was talking about John Cougar Mellencamp. Jesus probably agreed.

"I tried smoking," Cortney admitted, stirring the pool of paint. "At this party I went to."

"Oh, yeah?" I said looking up, careful not to suck in my breath.

"It didn't do anything to me," she continued, pressing the sponge gently onto her blue bedroom wall. "Not that I care if it did. It just makes you feel good." She pressed harder and harder. "And it's not like drinking, where you have to deal with sobering up. With smoking, at least you know what you're doing."

"Totally," I said, wondering what she meant.

Cortney eyed me, sensing that my heavenly ankle monitor was about to go off.

"Relax. I'm not a smoker. I don't want to hear about how bad it is for you either. Your lungs clean up after a few days."

I felt incredibly holy and insanely jealous at the same time. She was both drinking AND inhaling smoke? What next? Blow jobs? Being used? I shuddered, thinking about her poor, poor neglected future husband.

Ah, but imagine being used. Used . . . for sex. It was something happening on another planet, in a pamphlet filled with warnings. On my Earth, the only thing deep and penetrating was God's love.

"Steve's going to be at this party on Saturday." Steve: a senior and captain of the wrestling team. For Cortney, such stars were within reach.

"Really! That's awesome!" I said. Then I tried to appear thoughtful. "But what if he . . . if you drink, and he . . . *uses* you?"

"I know, I know. You don't approve."

"No, I just don't want you to get hurt."

I felt a strange lightness in my chest that I would later realize was the loss of my self-respect. Maybe Jesus was using *me*. Like a Muppet. And yet, I had to let Him. Because it was dangerous for my friend to be so guilt-free. Dangerous. Plus I didn't get to do any of that stuff. I soaked for a minute in my acute self-righteousness.

"I don't wanna wait to have sex," Cortney whined. "I know you're against it, but the way I was brought up, there's nothing wrong with it."

"No, it's not bad," I lied. Then I pictured me at a party, getting drunk and hooking up, but the scenario did not compute. I'd be in so much trouble, bad did not even describe how bad it would be. Mom would disown me, God would smite me, future husband would shame me. He'd get up sadly from our future candlelit table, walking away from me and my list of indiscretions forever. *I thought you were someone else,* he'd say, dropping his cloth napkin in a crumple at the base of the stemmed crystal.

Cortney stepped back to check her work. The effect was not as promised.

"This looks great," she said.

An angry thump came on her door. One of her brothers.

"Cort-ney . . ." he sang. "Are you guys naked?"

"Go away, you fucking asshole!" she screamed, chucking the wet sponge. It left a little white blob on her door. I stared, slack-jawed, at the indelible imprint of her dysfunctional family and also her apparent first-name basis with the word *fuck*.

Back at my house, God's own Partridge Family model unit, I realized it was up to me to save Cortney's endangered virginity, to pull her from the quagmire of her expletive-ridden and poorly sponged bedroom. I would do what I always did in a crisis: save souls. Via a five-hundred-word essay.

> *Dear Cortney,*
> *If you truly want to know that God is there, I believe you have to ask Him. Just say, "If you are truly there, God, then open my eyes." And He will. It will happen when you least expect it, and it will change your life. God can fill up the void in your life that Steve never can.*

But then again, I didn't have a Steve. It was much easier to fill up on God when you didn't have a popular athlete tantalizing you with his sweaty muscles. Plus I couldn't go to parties. I didn't want to. But that was because I wasn't invited. Which was God's Great Plan for my life. Earth sucked, I reminded myself, and the cost of getting into heaven was high. God had brought Cortney into my life so I could bring her closer to Jesus. The Lord was very mysterious.

It was made worse by my rampant, untreated addiction to large bangs and bathroom mirrors.

Though I had vowed that high school would be different, it really wasn't. Before school, between classes, before and after lunch, during study hall, and after school, I could always be found assuming the position by a bathroom sink, frantically doing my hair. Doing it, like a pimp pushing his ho. And as always, I continued to fail, on average, about eighteen times a day. For some odd reason, Cortney didn't want to spend high school panicking in the mirror with me. So when I got her note, I pretty much knew. I deserved it. God had probably ordained it.

> *I know you're probably mad at me for not hanging out. But you're always in the bathroom. I just hate standing in there waiting. I guess that's why I want to start giving our friendship some space. I don't want to be mad at you, and I hate going to the bathroom with you before and after lunch, and between every fucking class. How could hair be so important to you? I've tried to understand, but I still can't. I know your hair seems like a stupid reason for our friendship to be over, but that's all I can really think of.*

If she was the devil and I was Jesus, then clearly I had risen victorious. My virtue had prevailed, rising to the light like a corpse in deep water. But my social life had sunk straight down, down, down to the bosom of hell, where it came to a rest in the devil's ass crack.

After Cortney and I broke up, I went back to spending

more quality one-on-one time with my old friend, the tampon receptacle.

I started eating lunch in the bathroom because I couldn't just accept that my corresponding demographic was the nerd section, where girls used test scores and GPAs to establish their own subhierarchy and dominate each other like bull elephant seals in heat. It was far more comfortable being completely uncomfortable near anyone. Yea, I would deny-eth all social groups save the One True Group, a group I would quietly hate from afar, while eating a turkey sandwich in a stall.

I didn't end up there right away.

For a few days, when I exited the lunch line, I scanned the cafeteria for the ratio of bodies to empty chairs, frantic to locate the exchange students. So what if they wore scarves indoors and smelled funny? They were the equivalent of social Switzerlands because they had no past and no future, and would talk to anyone. But if there were no foreigners to be found, I had to sit alone. Sometimes Jimmy, the boy with Down syndrome, would sit in the empty seat next to me.

"Hi!" He'd smile, elated. "I love you!"

"I love you too, Jimmy," I said, feeling worthless. The cafeterial universe expanded all around us, an oppressing orbit of round tables, each one like an atom packed with the spinning electrons of friends tucked safely into their tightly packed nuclei. Jimmy beamed at me like he'd just seen the light, but I didn't know how to make conversation with him. I didn't really want to either, since I was on the verge of imploding. The vast, airless space of our empty table was condemnation. It was quarantine. It was nakedness. It was better to never step foot in here again.

The next day, desperate but nonchalant, I headed purposefully out of the cafeteria, no idea where I was going, hoping I was allowed to hide, hoping it was clear to onlookers that I wasn't going to go hide, no don't be ridiculous, I just had tons of busy and exciting things to take care of.

Cortney was sitting at a crowded table of hot upperclassmen and long-haired deadhead chicks. She was flanked by her new bestie, a girl so laid-back she seemed chronically high. Since I had forced Cortney to dump me, their new pastime had become laughing at me, which was possibly the worst thing ever in the history of worst things. As I strode past, I notched up my everything-is-going-great disposition, which wasn't easy to do when carrying a lunch tray into a locker room. I braced for their screeching laughter behind me, and it seemed to ricochet for miles.

It felt weird to sit on a toilet seat with pants on. But it was better than being stared at. I chewed my sandwich, trying not to look at the stained tile, while the three good fairies whizzed about my head, feeling sorry for me.

The poor dear! they cooed. *The little darling! Let's make her a cake. Make it blue! No, pink. Pink! No, make it blue!*

The door into the bathroom swung open. I picked up my feet and stopped breathing.

"This one's locked," a girl said, then whispered, "but there's someone in it."

Laughter.

"C'mon, hurry up and pee." They ignored my hiding and kept talking.

"Wait for me," said the other, going into the stall beside me.

"I can't. I gotta go!"

"Fine. Just go. I thought you were my friend. Fine."

"I have to go!"

"Go! Leave! I'll just mention a certain blow-job incident to a certain somebody."

Silence. A toilet flush.

"Look at you, you're stressing out. Ha-ha. Relax. I'm just kidding. But please, wait for me next time."

Blow jobs. They were everywhere. All the freshman girls around me, dropping like aliens in Galaga, shot down by the firing joysticks of hot, hard upperclassmen.

After school, in the locker room before basketball practice, I was privy to more and more secondhand sex. One of our starting forwards was Alyssa: tan, popular, sexy. She was the only one called "sweetheart" by our permanently angry coach. About every fifteen minutes he'd toss his clipboard down the suicide lines, disgusted beyond words. But Alyssa could chuck an airball and run into the wall and still be sweetheart.

"No, sweetheart. Arch your wrist."

"Sweetheart, come here."

"Grab the ball, sweetheart."

Then to me, eyes averted: "Hey! Get your head outta your ass!"

Alyssa pulled off her shirt by the row of lockers, and I stared with longing at the curve of her muscled legs. She was telling our point guard about her hot date, and I hung on every word as I dressed alone.

". . . He got on top of me," she whispered, "and he *wouldn't stop*! I was like, 'Oh my God.' After it was over, it felt like I had diaper rash."

"Oh my God, are you serious?" asked her friend. "That's so funny."

I looked up at my friend Mallory, who was lacing her

basketball sneakers on the bench next to me. We exchanged question marks. Diaper rash?

Alyssa giggled. "I could hardly walk."

Oh. They were *doing it.* Of course. That's why Coach liked her. It's a pheromone given off by penetrable females: *I might sleep with you too.* That's why her boyfriend kept being her boyfriend, month after month. Sex was the secret to dating longer than three minutes. Once you had sex with him, he'd follow you anywhere, even the mall. Like the guys you see sitting half-asleep in the armchairs by the ladies' fitting rooms. Like hungry, bored, whipped dogs. You could come to school looking like crap, with food in your teeth and wearing the same ugly pants as yesterday, and there he'd be, smiling with open arms, ready to give you more diaper rash.

"But she's only a freshman!" I whispered, wondering when it was exactly that I started speaking like my mom.

"Slut," whispered Mallory, pulling her shirt down over her sports bra before I could stare at her chest too, which for some reason I always found myself doing. "I'd never go all the way with Rob. I'd go to third, though."

"You'd let Rob . . . finger you?"

"Probably. Or your brother," she said with an evil laugh.

"Gross," I moaned. "I'd go to third when I'm, like, in college."

Mallory looked at me like I was crazy. "Hell, I'm not waiting that long."

But I had to wait. For me and God, sex was like a line at the deli. You don't ask questions, you take your number, starve, and hope you get called soon. And you spend Friday nights waiting with Jesus.

I pretended to go to bed. I lay there until my family was

asleep and the house was dark, and I crept down one stair at a time, avoiding all the creaky places, gliding so not even my knees cracked. I opened the screen door inch by inch, no sudden noises, and slipped out into the cold moonlight. I sat on the planks of the deck, with my headphones, and forwarded it to the right song, the one I picked out for God. "My life is for you," the song went, and I was the singer, my vibrato bursting like a bullet train of prayer, straight to the rafters of heaven. "Use me for your will!" Suddenly I was so important, so powerful, that I'd been transported straight to the front of the line, my face pressed against the glass ceiling of heaven. I was all up in the grill of Almighty God!

"Send help," I begged. "I really hate this place."

But the song ended and our bubble of communication burst. Silence rang in my ears.

God? Do you copy?

Restless, I turned off the tape and switched on the FM radio, spinning the dial slowly from 88.5 to 107.1, past static and classic rock and smooth jazz, waiting for my answer, like a satellite dish pointed out into space noise. I would know the answer by the words of a random song timed just so, telling me the plan for my life. God was so great, He could make fish and loaves out of the sad playlists of local Connecticut radio stations.

And sometimes, when it really worked, and my question was answered perfectly in the singing voice of Peter Cetera, I knew that Jesus could hear me. It was like my own private phone call to heaven. It was a high better than drugs. I mean, I wouldn't know for sure if it was better than drugs, but I did know I was getting drunk on *God,* an organic spiritual buzz, the way nature intended.

Those poor lost souls at Avon High School, missing out on the wonderful joy of their Blessed Redeemer, way down in the depths of their hearts!

You spend this much time with God, I imagined myself someday explaining to them, the throngs of the lost, *and your life is bound to get better!*

But that was only because things couldn't get any worse.

". . . her young breasts were crushed by the Egyptians."

—EZEKIEL 23:21

Monologue performance week in high school drama class was the ultimate power trip. We sat in the dark, and narrowed our keen eyes toward the stage, pencils poised on our comment cards.

Too much fidgeting, I wrote on one. *You abandoned your focus. Your accent does not sound English. The glasses look too feminine.*

The actor being scrutinized mumbled "scene" and his performance concluded, the class crackled with weak applause. *Too many props, too little subtext,* I thought to myself and passed my note card o' wisdom to the aisle. My stomach tied in delicious knots, awaiting my turn.

I was different. I was talented. I was gonna nail it. Jaws would drop, cheers would thunder, envy would reign.

You're gonna be famous!

Oh, stop, I'd gush.

The only teensy-weensy impediment to my amazingness

was memorizing lines. But what are lines really, mere words, when you have *talent*?

I stood onstage, holding my fist aloft, 1.21 gigawatts of drama quivering through my body, but my mind ticking on empty: line, line, line.

But I wouldn't give up. Not like the others. No. I was professional. There was no shame in calling for your line, so long as you stayed in character.

"Mother," I wept, brimming with the anguished subtext, "why did you . . . line . . ."

"Never," hissed the script holder.

"Mother! Why, why, WHY did you never . . . line . . ."

"Love me."

"*Love! Me!*" I breathed, in a dying stage whisper. "Line."

Afterward, in critique, our class would sit in a circle on the stage and take turns sharing what we thought of each other's performances, provided we didn't edit. Meaning we had to be brutally honest. But you couldn't just say it sucked. Even if it did. You had to state only what you *obseeerved* or how it made you *feeeel*.

Sometimes, it went something like this:

"I observed that you were really . . . unprepared."

"You're judging."

"I'm not judging, I'm observing."

"I observe that you are sometimes . . . hypocritical."

"I observe you are being rude. That makes me feel . . . like hitting you."

"Guys," said our teacher.

"I observe me observing you threatening me. And I'll FEEL happy when you get arrested for assault."

With so much drama and serious inner work going on

all around me, it was easy to fall in love with someone who loathed serious inner work. Someone like Liam, a freshman two years younger than me, but also a real living, breathing bona fide child actor.

I had never seen anyone who could ad lib like Liam. Sometimes when the teacher left, he'd chuck costumes, scripts, and pieces of plastic furniture offstage, rattling on in a dialect he'd made up off the top of his head.

"Who did that?" the teacher demanded, returning to survey the mess.

"Who did that?" Liam asked me calmly, his face right in mine. "Who did that?"

I pinched my nose and tried not to pee my pants.

Later in the costume closet, Liam would corner me, hanging a plastic wreath around his neck.

"My character needs to wear this," he'd plead. "Needs it. NEEDS. IT."

"Okay, but what's the subtext?"

"He was raped by a Christmas tree when he was five."

The constant laugh track of an older girl was an aphrodisiac for him. And I had never met a guy with intelligence and comic timing. Or ego. It made me swoon. Plus, he had that perennial baby face that all sitcom casting directors love. And once, a limo had picked him up in the roundabout at school.

"Big audition," he'd told me, before being whisked away to New York. I watched in awe.

Since he was too young to drive, he invited me over to his house one Friday evening. It was massive and modern, carved into the nouveau riche side of Avon Mountain, where there was not a vinyl-sided split-level in sight.

"You know I do commercials, right?" he said.

"Yeah," I purred. "Tell me more."

"You can tune in next Tuesday night for my cameo as a juvie on *Law & Order*."

"Wow!" I had no idea what a juvie was, or a *Law & Order*.

We shot pool downstairs, and I leaned over my cue stick as sensuously as I could, my wrists overwrought with tinkling fake gold bracelets. He dropped big, smoldering compliments.

"Those are really pretty."

"Shut up." I giggled.

Then we went for a walk so he could expound on the life and times of Liam. His loves, his hates, his hopes and dreams, his life on the silver screen, which would start any day now.

I watched him talking and fantasized about being his arm candy. It was a big dream, but I could practice in the mirror. This is me, waving good-bye as the limo whisks him to the studio. This is me, deferring to Liam when reporters ask questions. This is me, dabbing my eyes when he accepts the Academy Award.

But about a hundred feet into our walk, Liam pulled out a different persona in the shadows, along with a squashed pack of cigarettes.

"You smoke?" he asked, lighting one.

Oh, my gosh. I knew all the names of every disease that smoking could cause, but I'd never touched one. I would be brave now. I would take one. Like in the movies. Oh, things were about to look up for me.

He lit it for me and I tried to inhale but couldn't pull past the reflex in my trachea, handed it back coughing and teary-eyed. He blew rings over my head, huffing it down to a nub. I watched, amazed.

"What?" he said. "What?"

"Kiss me," I said, and braced for it, knowing that an actor, of all people, should know the cue for a love scene. But instead Liam collapsed at my feet in the road, arms sprawled, mouth open, like he'd been shot.

"Oh, my God, oh, my God." He laughed. "My God. That was perfect! Cut! Can you just say that, just one more time maybe?"

I couldn't believe he'd totally upstaged our love scene. But it wasn't my job to question. It was my job to be the best portable studio audience I could possibly be.

Driving home with the salty smell of tobacco on my fingertips, I wondered if I should give Liam something illegal of my own. Like my boobs. But tits were not like Marlboros. They had virtue attached to them, whereas cigarettes merely gave you bad breath.

Oh, he'd get them all right, but he'd have to wait. At least till maybe our fourth or fifth rehearsal. It was hard to say. He made me really hot.

The next weekend, we had our second date at my house. I got my love scene all right. We were kissing on the couch, ears pricked for the footfalls of my mother, and his thumbs started stroking me, right over the nipple. It was glorious, but no no no, NOT in God's script. I twisted away more than once.

"You're kidding," he said, sitting up.

"I'm sorry." I giggled nervously, not looking at him. "We haven't been going out that long."

"So, you don't . . . I can't . . . *what*?" he marveled, doing his trademark eyebrow lift.

"Well you know . . . when we've been together . . . for a while . . ."

I straightened up, gathering my mental flashcards from Bible class.

This was not the groupie he'd planned for. I looked into his lively eyes and realized the bulb inside his movie projector had snapped to off. Come Monday morning, I got a cheerful "hey" from him in the hallway, followed by "this isn't working out," and then, "we're becoming the people we swore we'd never be."

"Wait, what?" I asked.

"I'm sorry," he said, as our stage manager passed by him and snatched his ball cap.

"Hey!" he laughed, bounding off after her. "Bring that back!"

What he was trying to say to me was, in the biz, the supporting actress should oblige when the leading man cops a feel.

Argh! I had wanted to let him, wanted to so bad, but I just couldn't.

By seventh period I realized I had not only been dumped but also immediately replaced with said stage manager, who was a svelte, popular toy-size girl with hair bigger than her body.

I steeled myself as I opened the auditorium doors and made the dead man's walk to the stage. Liam was no longer funny. He was a shithead, and I missed him terribly. But the heavenly minions guarding my tiny sweater puppies had much rejoicing to do.

Liam and the stage manager paired up for the midterm exam to perform a scene from *Some Like It Hot*. I knew I was in for something bad as they swaggered up onto the stage. They lit cigarettes, which was really shocking of course, rattled off a few lines, then began making out frenetically, which was nothing short of epic and groundbreaking. Liam's hands grabbed her tiny rump and squeezed it for the audience, so we could all get a good look at him breaking off a piece. The teacher winced, the class snickered and cheered, scribbling reviews on their comment cards, and my head imploded quietly. I hunched over in the front row, 135 pounds of ungainly flab, penciling a dark, Saturn-shaped circle. *I observe your subtext is total asshole.* Then I tore up my card and stormed out.

Albeit unbearable, at least something was going on here. Something was actually happening in my life, and something was better than nothing. I immediately scrambled for another drama class boyfriend. Someone who could provide me with more manna from heaven, more of this life-sustaining drama.

There was one possibility: a pale, slightly gay-seeming upperclassman named Dante. My God, he even had a drama class name. I liked him because he liked me. I desperately liked being liked, especially in drama, where the stage manager was forever giving Liam erotic back massages before group.

Focusing on Dante's good parts—a nice smile at certain angles, lots of female friends—yeah, he was appealing, sort of. Sure, he was the skinniest, most easily pinned guy on the wrestling team, though he had dieted and sweated his way to the newborn class. It alternately pleased and pained me to watch his willowy ass pace the sideline at wrestling meets. It was like watching the boy version of myself, only worse, since he thought he was hot shit. After getting tossed out of the ring like a Frisbee, he would complain about the referee.

"That was cheap!" he'd seethe.

Yeah, cheap, I'd answer back, salivating for the husky firecracker who had trounced him. But I liked Dante. Or, I sorta liked him, I thought. Hey, we even had our own Sting song. And our own retarded handshake.

"The way you just smiled at me," he'd say. "That was way *blinky.*"

When things were good, they were not just good, they were "blinky." He stretched his lanky arm out to me for the signature move he'd created. He called it "twiddles"— curling his fingers and wiggling them with mine—which always had to accompany any blinky situation. Twiddles made me want to crawl into a hole and die, but it made Dante go goofy with happiness, so whatever. Twiddles.

My idea of a good date with Dante was lying back on the couch at his house, pretending to watch TV while he ran his hand up my thigh. I'd push it back down—no, no, *no,* I told him, *those* kind of twiddles are NOT blinky—though my crotch throbbed and my panties dripped for more. No doubt future husband would ask for a full write-up on this event, and would be so pleased. But my tightly clamped legs drove Dante up the wall.

"Do you want to know what would be really blinky?" he breathed into the phone one night.

"What," I asked, dreading, excited, ready for the Test.

"If when we're making out, you would kiss my stomach and then put your head down lower, unbutton my jeans, and . . ."

"Mm-hm?" I carried the phone casually and quickly into an empty room.

"And go even lower . . . and pull down my boxers . . . and put your *mouth* on it. That would be sooo blinky."

Silence.

"I think you'll really like it, trust me," he said, breathing hard.

Reams of prerecorded excuses scrolled through my mind, too fast to pick. I stared out the dark window at the lone streetlamp. In the next room Mom rummaged in a kitchen cupboard.

"Know what?" he said, trying a different tack. "If you liked me, you'd do it."

"We've only been going out for like two weeks," I said.

"I think you just don't like me."

Oh, crap. I never wanted anyone to think I didn't like them. Then they might not like me back! And people liking me back was the only fuel source I was designed to run on.

"Just because I don't want to do that doesn't mean . . . I mean, of course I like you!"

"Well then why wouldn't you do that? Aren't you my girlfriend?"

I thought: Sucking dick is supposed to be special. We needed to get to know each other. I'm worth waiting for. Jesus loves me, this I know. Blah, blah, blah. The truth was Dante's penis—perhaps because it was attached to Dante— was sort of icky. It was much easier to just get titillated by his hands persisting up my thighs.

At our next couch date, Dante tried Plan C. It was very subtle. While we were kissing, he applied gentle pressure to the top of my head as one might a Pez dispenser. He was trying to train my face to find his dick. When that didn't work, he sat up and ignored me, flipping the TV channels. Oh no. I was going to get dumped again.

As a last resort, Dante sent his platonic female assistant Brittany to call me later that week. The news was out: Dante had deemed me a prude. *Prude,* that was his dad's word, you could so tell. Dante's dad was in the stands sweating bullets at all his wrestling meets, anxious to score his son a victorious heterosexual encounter before it was too late.

"I just thought you should know," Brittany said, and I could tell instantly she was jealous that Dante had never asked her to kneel 'n' bob.

"Just because I don't want to do certain things," I told her, "doesn't mean I'm, like, frigid."

Frigid. I was not frigid. Frigid people were afraid of sex. They hated sex, whereas I longed for any possible kind of sex, just not real sex, not until my future husband, or a stunning carbon copy of one, had come on the scene, pun intended in Jesus's name.

"You have to at least take off your shirt," Dante explained on yet another phone call. "Otherwise . . ." I waited through the long pause. "Otherwise I don't know where this is going."

I wasn't stupid. I'd been down this road with Liam. I knew I couldn't cut him off and have nobody liking me. Then what? Return to my depressing life on the back porch with Jesus? I hadn't put up with blinky and twiddles all this time for nothing. I'd have to play the tit card. It was time. I tried to psych myself up by thinking about how jealous Brittany would be. I wasn't desperate. Desperate? *Me?* Please. I was just so excited for him. Sure, he sucked at sports and was so cheesy it sometimes scared me, but he could forever polish the metaphorical crown he would earn as the First Guy to See My Tits. I was ready to bring the burnt offering. All we needed was an altar.

On the next date, Dante parked his blue Volvo in the moonlight and we cut through the woods to the top of an overlook and paused. The lights of houses twinkled below.

"Now this," he said, "this is way blinky. Twiddles."

I agreed. This was not cheap and seedy, but lo, ripe with heavenly meaning. In the splendor of the full moon, with angels singing soprano and rapidly rising to a crescendo, I prepared myself to sin lightly. We kissed for a few minutes, then I unbuttoned my blouse, revealing a frilly new Maidenform (carefully selected) while Dante fell to his knees in worship.

I unlatched the clip and let it slide off.

"Blinky!" came his muffled cries as he covered his face with my 34Bs. My God, I thought, looking down. Manna to a starving man. And to think I harvested these little pied pipers without sit-ups, makeup, magazine how-tos, or any brain power whatsoever. Straddling his bony frame, we made out until making out was not enough, and he educated me in undulating together through jeans.

"Dry humping," he whispered.

Dry humping, I thought. Like a kind of dog food. But soon the genius behind the disgusting term was revealed. This was sterile, guilt-free sex—no groping, no nudity, *no sin*! Good old-fashioned galloping and grinding, like grandma used to make. There weren't even bases associated with this, the outfield of sexual dog chow. La-di-da, don't mind me, just riding along on the lump in his jeans, until *boom,* it hit me. It happened.

Maybe we did it for too long, or maybe it felt too good, but suddenly my gyrating hips started thrusting completely out of my command, like I was being remotely controlled, or sucked into a vortex, a black hole, a swirling pleasure so all consuming it annihilated my ability to think or care about anything. Blasting upward like a rocket, I scrambled off his lap, terrified that I'd snapped my spinal cord in half.

"Whoa." I breathed, panicking to count my fingers and toes.

"What's wrong?"

"Nothing!" I whisper-screamed, groping around in the grass. "I'm fine! Something happened! Felt like I . . . like I almost *died*!"

"Blin-ky." Dante sighed, sounding bored. He was splayed on the ground with his yet unopened boxers puffing out of his unzipped jeans.

"Wow." I looked up at the stars. "Wow, oh my gosh! I guess that's . . . what *sex* is like!"

Dante sat up. "So you like it? You want to try it now?"

I looked at him, then covered my semiexposed tits. They had bought me like, what, five minutes?

"Lemme work up to it," I said.

But a blow job was definitely not on the menu. I stalled, and within two weeks I found my severance package from Dante waiting in my locker, folded origami-style.

I hope you realize there won't be a perfect guy trotting toward you on a white horse to sweep you off your feet, only me. I know I'm not everything you want in a guy, but you're not everything I want in a woman, so what? The special thing we have (that makes marriages work) is our friendship.

His dad had written that, I was pretty sure. "Girlfriend" meant obliging dick sucker, and "friendship" was the golden ticket to the next wrestling tournament, and the exclusive honor of watching him get snapped like a spandex-covered toothpick.

The letter went on:

What's worse? You need my friendship as much as I want you to be my girlfriend.

Love,
Your "friend" Dante

I sat down and worked on two or three revisions of my response, making sure every word was perfect, and my handwriting was perfect, and the paper was perfect, in case he wanted to worship it later, perhaps use the corners to dry his tears. I told him how important our friendship was and that we should build on that before orally exploring the wonderful world of Girlfriend.

Dante's response, shoved into my hand in the hallway, was scribbled on the corner of a dirty cafeteria napkin.

Fine, I see we're no longer blinky. But my hormones told me to give it a try. I was very attracted to you, but I think I'm over that now. No hard feelings?

All the wind in my sails died. The prom. My fear of wet humping, noncanned variety, had cost me the ticket to his senior prom. Oh, no. Not prom. Dante wasted no time awarding it to some other girl who gave him unlimited helpings of head between class. Twiddles.

How could he have gotten over me and my tits so quickly? Just a short while ago, he worshipped them as gods. And now: a dirty napkin in my hand. I bet Jesus and His Heavenly Eunuchs didn't have any "hard" feelings about it. It was their business to be soft.

I hadn't even liked Dante, and look, the whole thing had backfired. But, whatever. My misery would be all the more appreciated by stupid future husband.

Oh, but Dante—sniff—*Dante was gone!*

After school, on the bus ride to benchwarm another basketball game, I slumped in the front seat, drying my eyes with his note. Alyssa passed down the aisle to take her seat in the back, with all the other pretty cocksuckers, and I pined for her hair, her life. If I'd been pretty like that, Dante might have stayed around to love me, even with my legs crossed and his dick unsucked.

Now it was back to my old life where, ironically, I would spend most of my time sucking.

My schedule was a veritable cornucopia of pure, un-mitigated suck. I continued to suck generously at both the violin and the piano, I sucked at basketball and volleyball, I had also joined track so I could suck at throwing a discus. I made sucky vegan brownies for the Animal Rights Club suck sale. Then, for shits and giggles, I joined the Amnesty International club so I could sit in the back and discreetly suck at picking my nose. And as I shuttled from one extra-curricular suckfest to another, gathering little Reese's Pieces for my future college résumé, my mother never suspected that secretly I would've let all these spinning plates fall and crash. I would've pimped out my soul and sold my own mother for one shot at the single thing I couldn't even fess up to wanting. It was called an orgasm. But I didn't know what it was called. In my mind, it was that thing that happened by accident, back on the cliff with Twiddle-dick.

As far as I knew, this urgent, epic quest required a boy. It could not be practiced. It could not be scheduled. It existed within the confines of the word *boyfriend,* and then, only after you'd vetted him, teased him, and tested his resolve for months—or days, depending on how hot he made you— until finally you accidentally gyrated on him at a certain angle for a little too long and: *boom.* You'd go unconscious with pre-Rapturized bliss.

But now at least I had gleaned two important pieces of data about myself. 1) I was willing to suck dick, but 2) I was not willing to suck Dante's dick. In order to suck a guy's dick, he had to be hot. Although what "hot" was, I wasn't sure. It was very subjective. Any guy could be good-looking, but he didn't activate into Hot until you caught him being nice to you. From there, it would attack your heart like fire ants on a half-baked worm.

It was the way he talked, the way his clothes hung, a chance sighting in the hall that would ignite days of swooning.

I waited and watched for Hot, anxious.

Then Trent showed up in drama one day, but only to get out of taking a class he hated even more.

The white-bread crowd steered clear of Trent since he showed up daily with unpleasant variations to his body, homemade piercings, a Mohawk, HATE Sharpied on his knuckles, his pants razored off at the knee. He had painted the symbol for anarchy on his army backpack, which he wore over his chest like a baby carrier: ta-da, the principle in action. He was too troubled to do anything fake, like lift weights or do sports. But when he smiled at me one day, with that brooding demeanor and those muscled forearms and big, square, scarred-up fists, one thing began to pulse in my diminutive brain: Hot.

He was not soft core, no, he was forced entry. I imagined him bullying me into submission and ravaging me against my will. It wouldn't be my fault. Yay! Then later, when we were done making out, my Christlike nature could bring him closer to a life full of kindness and meaning.

Trent seemed to be in favor of shooting humans, but he loved animals. He showed up to a few of our animal rights club meetings, which consisted of me and a bunch of depressed, oversensitive girls who related to anything trapped and abused. Trent sat there on the counter, saying nothing, chewing the wire of a paper clip.

He noticed me noticing him. He'd go out of his way to be extra obnoxious, tripping some freshman while I watched.

"Watch out for my shoe, asswipe." Then he'd grin at me.

I'd never once been on the winning end of a bully's power trip. It was fucking heady.

I welcomed his company into the Dante-Liam void of drama class. Trent was the antidote to blinkiness. Even serial-killer creepy was better than lame-wrestler-pussy boy. Even though I'd given him the blinkiest night of my life, damn it.

At least in drama class I could count on the dim lighting in the auditorium, which helped render my face 40 percent less visible when Dante walked in with his new girlfriend, flushed from fellatio. Then came Liam, carrying the stage manager's ass over his shoulder, making her laugh like crazy. God, they were all so attractive and happy. I sunk deeper into my chair, longing to evaporate.

Then came Trent, last as always, meandering down the aisle toward the stage. He sat directly behind me and propped up his feet by my head. He wore red-and-white-striped suspenders pinned to camouflage pants, and weathered, black Doc Martens that pined to kick a child actor's head in. I was his polar opposite, a heavily permed Christian wearing printed leggings from a clearance rack at the Limited.

"How's Dante?" he asked me. I turned to look at him and that wide, fake grin. Real grins, of course, were for posers.

"Shh," I said.

"Oh, look!" Trent yelled, ignoring me. "There he is! Your old boyfriend! With the girl you got ditched for!"

Dante looked over at us and I died. Whereas Trent lived for awkward confrontations, I lived to hide from them. I slumped over and pretended to look through my book bag.

"Trent!" I hissed. "Shh!"

"Quit being a dick," Dante called back.

"What did you say?"

"You're a dick, Trent." Dante slung his bag down next to an empty row of seats.

"Oh, Dante," moaned Trent, like he was jacking himself off. "Y'know I think I'd enjoy beating the fucking shit out of you."

"Try."

"Oh, you mean that?" Trent was suddenly all business, crackling his knuckles and sending a ripple through HATE. A few people hushed and looked over. There was a pause as Dante stared him down, reviewing the possibility of his swollen and disfigured prom picture, his dad's disappointment.

"Dude," he said, shaking his head in disbelief, "chill."

Then he sat down like it didn't matter, but you could tell. It was total submission.

"You kids have fun now." Trent chuckled.

I was nearly breathless. He'd said "fucking shit"! I longed to put it on playback, especially the part where Dante pretended not to be scared. It was awful, awful stuff, and oh—there it was, right there: I burned with the pleasure.

After school in the parking lot, Trent screeched over in a beat-up black hooptee and asked if I wanted to go over to his dad's apartment. Apartment? People in Avon didn't have apartments.

"Sure. I've just got to run to my locker," I told him, then ran to the pay phone to get permission from my mom.

"You've got a project?" Mom asked.

"Yeah, just an hour or two and we'll be done."

Mom was trusting. She knew I had a thing for Jesus.

In the passenger seat I looked at his wrists resting on the top of the chewed-up steering wheel, a cigarette dangling in his fingers. He was almost two years older, but it seemed like ten. He caught me looking at him and pointed back at me, like I had just done something hilariously stupid.

"What?" I asked.

"Nothing."

At his disheveled, parent-free, and decidedly nonsuburban digs in the neighboring town, he showed me a photo album of him and his skinhead friends, all wearing armbands and doing the *heil* Hitler.

"We're the *new* skinheads," he assured me. "It has nothing to do with being racist or any of that. It's about ska. And animal rights."

I flipped through page after page of eerie group photos of Trent and his skinhead friends posing in front of a big red-and-black swastika, looking like they were in a trance. He watched my muted horror with an aw-shucks grin.

"Don't look so worried," he said, ruffling my nonmoving, oversprayed hair, which now probably looked ridiculous. Trent didn't notice. He leaned back and began to detail the fighting scars on his hands.

"This one's from when I beat my dad with a beer bottle. And this over here is when he burned me back with his cigarette." I wondered if I should believe him, or if this was Trent's version of foreplay. Any minute he was either going to kiss me or kill me. What would I do? Act normal? I stood up and walked over to the tanks of reptiles stacked by the window. It was dark outside and the fluorescent lights glowed purple.

"Something is wrong with his skin," Trent muttered over the iguana, for a moment seeming soft. "My brother didn't take care of him."

Silence passed, and he stepped closer, like it was time. He was going to do something wonderful and severe to me. I waited for it to pass, and unfortunately it did—he jammed his fists into his tight pants, two taut notches on his hips. Saved. Darn it.

"Yeah, well, I gotta go home," I said.

"Yeah, I know," he said, picking up his keys. "Need a ride?" His tone had changed.

"Yeah."

"No, I mean on my big, throbbing dick."

Shocked, I rolled my eyes like I'd heard that one before. I hadn't.

"It is really big," he said as we walked out to the dark parking lot.

"I know, you told me."

"Wanna see?"

"No, no, I don't," I said, not even considering if maybe I did.

He swerved out of the drive, speeding full throttle all the way, running red lights and passing over the double yellow.

"Trent," I murmured, wondering if I would die. He raced down my quiet neighborhood street and passed my drive-way. He put the car in reverse and swerved in backward, idled, and looked at me, eyes twitchy and wide. I went for the door but he flipped the locks down. We stared each other down.

"So," he said, "what do you want me to do?"

"Uh," I said.

"Do you want me to kiss you?" he said, not sweetly. "What do you want me to do? Should we have sex before you go?" A crooked grin. "In the back? Fuck you hard?"

Whoa. That was inappropriate. That was awesome.

"Um, no thanks." I laughed, like we were making small talk. My hand was on the door latch. "Are you like trapping me?"

He stared.

"Bam, bam, bam," he teased, banging his fist into the socket of his palm. I watched his hands the way a deer watches headlights. "What?" He smiled, like this was so stupid.

"Trent," I said.

"WHAT THE FUCK YOU WANT ME TO DO?"

When I said nothing, he grabbed my head and filled my mouth with his teeth and his wagging, violent tongue, lock-ing my head in place with his arm. His other hand clamped down on my bra—total domination, so not Harlequin

Romance. Interesting. I imagined my face on the TV screen, face blurred out to protect my identity.

Did you lead him on?

No, I don't think so. I mean, it all happened so fast.

I pictured Trent mounting me, pinning my hands back while he ripped my shirt off with his fangs, whipping out his oversize dick and ramming it in. Like the rape scene on *Guiding Light* where I had secretly rooted for the attacker, which of course I knew was wrong, wrong and perverted. But I liked the way he commanded her to strip, and she obeyed tearfully, slipping off her top, her bare back to the cameras. "Please!" she begged. "Don't do this." And then, of course, the Lysol commercial. But before I could beg Trent not to do anything that exciting to me, someone flipped the floodlights on over the driveway, as if from God's very own watchtower. He let me go, erupting into laughter.

"Just kidding!" he screeched. "Ha-ha, look at your face!"

I got out, angry and ready to brag to someone, anyone, about crazy Trent. He had, like, almost *raped* me! His car peeled away, leaving me breathless.

Trent left me alone after that. And back in drama class, Jimmy joined the cast. He had a part as the grandfather clock in the spring play.

"Dong! Dong!" he bellowed.

"Awesome job," everybody cheered, overcompensating just a tad.

As usual, Jimmy was my number one fan. Whenever I walked in, he ran to me with his arms outstretched, calling my name so loud it echoed through the auditorium.

"Jimmy!" I shouted, as he swallowed me up in a powerful hug, knocking the air out of my lungs.

"She's my girlfwend," he announced, and stood there, beholding me with abject happiness. "My *girlfwend*."

While the class sighed with a collective "aw!" I squirmed in my shoes, flattered and afraid. I took my seat next to him in group anyway, and accepted my fate. At least he was nice to me. At least he wasn't a dipshit. And with Jimmy's platonic love restored, maybe my breasts were finally safe, commended unto the eager and omnipotent bosom-loving hands of our Lord and Savior, Jesus Christ.

10 | In Wondershorts We Pray

> "They saw he was a comely babe, and
> they feared not the king's edict."
>
> —HEBREWS 11:23

The real and true test of my acting ability was not going to be on a stage at my high school drama class. It was going to be on the beach. Right before our family's annual summer trip to south Florida, I got a stomach flu that nearly killed me, but left me conveniently emaciated. Thin! And sixteen! In Florida! If I pulled this off, I had a second shot at starring in a commercial for the American dream. It would last about three days.

But who cared about the inevitable plateau and spiral? *I've got God on my side,* I wrote in my journal in big, loopy girl cursive. My handwriting seemed to match the dimming wattage of my brain. *I feel so close to Him these past few days. God, thank you. Thank you for healing me. I thank you for your compassion, your understanding, your love.*

What I meant was, thank you for making me throw my guts up. But I loved kissing God's ass with flowery love letters, especially when I didn't have to practice violin or piano for two whole weeks. Yesss.

I learned an important lesson that summer. Anyone—*anyone* with a head—could pass for hot, so long as you have an excuse to feel the part, and your audience is mainly composed of drunk frat guys. None of the hunks on the beach knew that fifteen hundred miles away someone was probably drawing a goatee on my yearbook photo. If I could convincingly play the role of cheerleader, then maybe, just maybe, Jesus would let me hook up with a real live football player.

At high noon I sat in my beach chair at the water's edge and slipped my toes into the warm, lapping waves. I splashed water on my boobs, smeared oil on my thighs, stretched out my newly visible rib cage, and scanned for the hottest guy I could find. There was a slew of college-aged studs playing beach volleyball, and one of them drew my gaze like a magnet. He was the human equivalent of a Dove Bar, with short black hair and shoulders that swelled above his waist. The more I watched him spike and dive, the more completely beautiful and unattainable he became. It was hard to look away. I held up my book to suggest that I was reading. Then I glanced down at the sun shining on my boobs. The ocean sparkled for miles, and a few yards to my right young men grunted and sweated and flexed. For an hour, I was the Eye of Providence atop the magic triangle—bronzing boobs, brimming waves, black-haired stud. I could've stayed there all day. I could've stayed there for the rest of my life.

Then someone served the volleyball out-of-bounds at high velocity and it came rolling right over to me, where it bobbed in the shallow water at my feet. I froze. Holy crap.

My stud was jogging over to get it. Within seconds, he was right in front of me, striding into the waves, bending to splash sand off the ball. Shocked, I dropped my paperback into the water. I reached in to fish it out, realizing in a millisecond that (a) his shorts were soft like sweatpants, (b) I had just rendered my prop/book unusable, and (c) I was slapping and clawing my arms like I had a nerve disorder. My fingernails left little white lines in my sunburn.

"You okay?" he asked, pausing to watch me.

"Bugs!" I blathered. "They're eating me alive!"

Wait, *what*? What did I just say?

"I've got some spray," he said kindly. "Want me to get it?"

He was shirtless. Shirtless in a way that numbed my mind. He had tan freckles, just a few, on the bridge of his nose. He had some kind of tough-sounding accent, picked up from the faraway land of Hot Guy. Boston maybe. Or Philly.

"Yeah," I said, confused by the rampant stupidity of my speaking voice. "I mean no, I'm okay! But thanks!"

Stupid! I thought as I watched him saunter away. *Stupid!* If bugs were actually biting me, it would've been *in character* to say yes. Why would I have said no? *Stupid!* Only a demented masochist would say no to a blatant act of kindness. Ugh. Dork. If he ever offered me anything ever again, I vowed, even if it was a slap upside the head, I would say YES YES and YES bring it ON.

I packed up my chair and retreated to our condo on the top floor. It had a rooftop balcony, and with our family binoculars (voyeurism was an important part of our annual tradition) I could spy on him to my heart's content. I scanned the beach and zeroed in on the volleyball court, but a cluster of palm trees kept getting in the way. I watched and waited, waited and watched, and finally he emerged with some kid, maybe his little brother. They were throwing a ball back and forth as they jogged along the grassy path. As they passed by below me, I leaned over the rail to zoom in. From this bird's-eye view, you could see all kinds of things you normally couldn't. Like, for instance, the shape of his dick swinging back and forth in his soft shorts. Yup, there it was. Holy crap. Sweet Lord above. God almighty.

It wasn't even icky. It was the absolute opposite of icky. Angels sang before it. Jesus wept.

That night's journal entry, I wrote one line: *Thank you, God. Florida is like HEAVEN.*

After a few days of trying to find an in with the one I had knighted Sir Wondershorts, I discovered the missing link to popularity. It was beer. When hot guys drink beer, they will talk to anybody.

Late one night, I found him with his college crew, drinking Michelobs out of a cooler at the condo pool. They were playing a raucous game of volleyball in the shallow end. I knew all this before I even got there because, like Jane Goodall, I had my binoculars pressed against our screened-in porch, studying their complex social behaviors and erratic migration patterns.

It was time for some hands-on field research.

Quickly, I reapplied my makeup, drenched my neck in perfume and my hair in conditioner, leaped into my bathing suit so fast I nearly ripped off the straps, and raced down three flights to the pool. As I approached I became slow, demure, and nonchalant. Casual-like, I stopped to take in the wonder of a palm tree. I paused to consider an ant on the railing. *Hello, fellow traveler.* Then, I made my red carpet entrance at the pool, perched on the ledge and dipped my feet in. *Just here to swim,* said my laid-back body language. *It's a free country, right?*

My plan was to relax, and pass the time as all wannabe blonds do, staring directly into shiny lights. And also pondering this one particular muscle on Wondershorts's body. Later, I would dig through an anatomy book until I located the word for the burn between my legs: *deltoids.*

"Hey," someone called out to me, snapping my trance.

It was Wondershorts. Talking. Talking to me. With words.

I stared.

"Would you mind being our referee? The pool is full of CHEATERS."

His voice was low and hoarse. Scruffy. The kind of voice that made you want to cover yourself in cooking oil and piña colada concentrate, and present yourself as a nubile sacrifice to the volcanic gods of beach sex.

"Me?" I said, almost swallowing my tongue. "Sure, I'll ref."

"What?" laughed his friend. "What? Who's cheating?"

"Dude. We need a ref."

I had an hour and a half till curfew. I also had Mom sitting in a chair on the screened-in porch, pointing her binoculars directly at my back.

The game resumed with me somehow miraculously included. One of them reached up to slam the ball. It slipped just over his fingertips and he came down with a huge splash.

"Touched it!" someone yelled. "He touched it!"

"Did not!" He laughed.

Then they began water wrestling. It was like rabid,

breaching whales. Only they were tan and glistening, with dark, firm nipples.

"Ref!" Wondershorts called over the tumult. Two others waded over to me, so close to my legs I could reach out and lick them.

"You saw that, right?" one of them said, breathing hard.

"Hmm," I said, grinning. "What?"

"If it's in, you can have a beer."

The other: "It was out. And we'll give you a case to prove it."

Wondershorts hung back a bit.

"Guys," he said, laughing, "c'mon. She's a baby. How old are you, sweetheart?"

"Sixteen." I smiled at him. "Y'know. Like *Princess Aurora*."

"Huh?"

He'd called me *sweetheart*. And *baby*. Oh, sweet Lord above, Christ almighty, God help me. Oh Jesus! Oh Jesus Jesus Jesus! I love Jesus!

"How old are *you*?" I stuttered.

"Twenty-one."

If only I had a camera, to prove this was actually happening. I had friends. Hot older guy friends who liked me. Oh, my goodness, I wanted to move here! We'd all become close and live in the same neighborhood and marry each other and our kids would play ball together and live happily ever after because Florida was a-MAZ-ing!

Wondershorts looked right at me and flashed a gorgeous smile. I, on the other hand, had no idea what my face was doing.

"How about you forget the beer," he said. "If it's out, you can just have me for the whole night."

The catcalls erupted. The tiki torches went out of focus. He liked me. He liked me. *The world,* a voice in my head whispered, *the world has been set aright.*

"That's it," yelled another, hopping out. "Beer break!" Then to me: "Want one?"

There was some other dude on my left, hoisting himself to sit next to me on the ledge.

"I'm Josh," he said, dripping on me. "Where you from?"

"No thanks. I'm drunk," I lied, staring at them all. "I'm from Connecticut."

"All of us and one drunk chick," he scolded. "Trouble."

"Jail bait."

I could have any guy on either team. I could pick A, B, or C, or just E and F. Any combination thereof. But I only wanted the alpha. I wanted Wondershorts, who was now getting out of the pool and heading for the hot tub. Without me. My heart sank. He sauntered past me and paused. I looked up at his wet body, slick hair, the grin still playing on his full lips. His thumb was resting on his hip, just above the waistband. With his other hand he beckoned.

"Wanna come?" he asked.

And yea, the light shoneth down from heaven and the heavenly hosts did sing greatly.

"Be right back," I told what's-his-name beside me. As I reared back to do a running slide into the hot tub, which was conveniently out of binocular range, my sister suddenly appeared in dry clothes, like a boom box mangling my Bel Biv DeVoe tape. Her eyes conveyed a clear message: *Virginity at Risk.*

"Why are you here alone?" she asked. "These guys are total . . . dicks."

"It's okay," I said, shocked that she had said *dicks* out

loud. We were so not in Kansas anymore. I used her as cover as I shifted my boobs around for maximum bustiness. "I'm totally fine. You can go back to the room."

"I wouldn't trust these dudes as far as I could throw them. Plus"—she sighed—"Mom told me to come get you."

"No!"

"Just hurry up and come."

"What?"

"You have to come in."

"Oh okay, just a sec," I said, almost knocking her down.

Just a sec? Hurry up? I had no intention of doing that. This was not swimming laps. This was not practicing the goddamn piano. This was my life-or-death shot at being Sleeping Beauty.

"Be right there," I called back to her.

My sister, possibly inoculated by all the airborne testosterone, became part of the backdrop and I sank into the hot water with Wondershorts.

"Looks like Sean's outta the game," said someone far, far away. The bubbles churned and steamed around us, much like the molten lava feeling in my crotch, much like the Lake of Fire that corresponded to this situation in the afterlife.

"I'm Sean." He grinned.

"Hi, Sean. Nice to meet you. So, where you from?"

"Philly."

"Oh. Philly. I like your accent."

"Thanks." He laughed softly.

I moved closer to him, so he would know. He said nothing, reading me. Then he ran his hand along my forearm under the water. Such a light touch for such a big guy. We were making conversation about something, I think, but I was distracted. My body had just been plugged into a wall socket in the general area of my vagina, and the circuit board was about to fry. I looked up at him and held his gaze, just long enough to signal a kiss. And with my sister filling in for my conscience, leaning on a bored elbow under the tiki torches, I got to find out what it was like to French kiss a wet, hot guy. I pressed my lips to his and caressed his neck and hair. Soft tongue, hard shoulders, and he smelled like lotion. Better than any dessert I'd ever tasted. I pulled his head into mine. I wanted to tell him with my tongue how agonizing it was to look all week, all my life, and never touch. I ran my fingers down his chest and up his sides, making him breathe harder, his finger hooked around the bikini strings at my hip.

"Do you want to take a walk?" he whispered, looking past me. The other guys were watching him get me, the coveted prize, and this I found pleasingly in line with National Geographic animal shows. Sean seemed to like it slightly less. "Let's go somewhere private."

"Private," I repeated, dazed. "Sure." We stepped out, steaming from head to toe, and made a beeline for our towels. He toweled off, grabbed his room key, and put on some bug spray.

"Got some if you need it." He smiled, holding up a can of *Off!* I sucked in my breath: oh! It was our first inside joke!

"Be right back," I said to my sis as we passed. "He just wants to go look for sea turtles! Really superquick!"

"Wait!" she hissed.

"Tell Mom we're looking for *sea turtles!*" I reminded her.

Sea turtles. Two feet out of sight we were on top of each other, sucking each other's faces. He was trying to slip his hands inside my bikini, which would have been marvelous, only I couldn't let it be marvelous.

"Just one thing," I breathed, pulling away from his glorious tongue. "Not here [breasts] or here [crotch], okay?"

He stared at me, needing a review, but I attacked his body, tangling my legs with his in the sand, straddling the hard-on in his swim trunks like a human C-clamp. When you sit on someone, I reasoned, it's touching by accident. No foul. I began galloping feverishly toward the horizon, while Sean's hands stopped obediently short of my end zones.

"You know," his voice was muffled in my neck, "I know we wouldn't ever do . . . *that*."

"No, never," I replied, biting his ear and gyrating harder.

"No, of course, never, I would never, but if we did? I think I'd want to lose it with you."

I paused. I sat back to look at him in the dark.

"You're a virgin?" I asked.

"Yeah, is that okay?"

I went slightly cross-eyed. He was pure. Well, allegedly. Highly unlikely, but it was an excellent tactic, really. Excellent. I immediately considered letting him go to second base. While I pondered this I sucked his tongue deep into my mouth, wondering how deep it could go, then slid downward so I could lick him from neck to navel to nipple and to . . . what? Hmm, what was that, that *taste*? Horrid, chemical, burning . . . sort of like, oh no. Like DEET. Instantly my entire mouth went numb and I finally understood, with grave certainty, that tonight was the last night of my life. I was about to die of toxic shock syndrome.

I pulled away, bent over, and commenced spitting in the sand. I spit and spit, hocking loogies and wiping my mouth with the back of my hand. The numbness spread to the inside of my cheeks. I was definitely going to die, but first I would probably have a seizure and then go into a coma.

"You okay?" he asked, sitting up on an elbow. I hacked and retched some more, then staggered away toward the lights of the pool to find water and medical attention.

This has been a test of the Lord's Emergency Abstinence Protection System. We had to poison her to save her eternal soul. Should this have been an actual emergency, you would have totally scored. Oh, well.

Hours later, back in the condo, I could feel my tongue again and I was still alive. But I was aching, wet, and tense everywhere else. I curled up around my journal.

Oh God, I wrote. *Jesus, I love you, you're the man I need to be with. You're my first priority.*

I turned off the light and lay awake, staring into the dark, thinking about what had just happened.

Was it me?

Couldn't have been. There were no other girls to choose from. I just got lucky.

I won him. I was beautiful.

You got a tan. They were drunk.

Not just the tan. Not just the beer.

They haven't even seen how your body looks when you actually eat food.

He was the most beautiful man ever. I was good enough for him.

Well, back to school now. Back to Ugly Girl.

Yeah, but still. You can't make me forget. When I'm not at school, I'm a completely different girl.

11 | The Art of Sucking

"I have gotten a man with the help of the Lord."

—GENESIS 4:1

At the end of my junior year in high school, I papered my bedroom with Greenpeace magazines and NARAL posters and pro-choice banners and petitions to protect the fur seals and the North American cougar. SAVE THE HUMANS, my posters proclaimed. I looked at the photo of Earth from space and felt a surge of righteous pity.

Though I couldn't relate to being violent, I had grown to hate all earthly powers that be. And since I couldn't throw red paint on the white strapless dresses of the homecoming court, hating the Republican Party was the next best thing. How dare they reverse pollution standards and protections for fluffy, endangered animals and force women into back-alley abortions! The nerve! I mean, even though I was saving myself for marriage, what would happen if I got raped? The only old white man who could tell me what to do with my body was God. And I was entirely confident the only rape-baby the Lord wanted me to carry was my future husband's.

Problem was, I'd never actually met a card-carrying member of the Republican Party who was friendly. Or gorgeous. I didn't know such a creature existed. I thought they were born smug and bald and with lopsided mouths.

One Friday night, I borrowed Dad's car and took two Estonian exchange students (the only friends who would go anywhere with me) to T.G.I. Friday's.

While we sat in our booth making halting small talk with nods and hand gestures, some guys kept sticking their heads through the plastic plant canopy and leering at us.

One snickered. "Are you gonna eat that?"

I looked at him to see if this was playful or mean. They seemed pretty dumb actually, but in the farthest seat, one of them smiled apologetically. Strong jaw, light eyes, nice hair, polo shirt. I smiled back, wondering what the hell was wrong with him.

"American guys are idiots," I said to my Estonians, who looked at me blankly. Then we got our check and left.

"Hey!" someone called to us in the parking lot. We turned around to see the nice-looking preppie boy catching up to us.

"My name's Alex," he said. "Where you guys from?"

"Yes, thank you," said Orla, still practicing English.

"I'm sorry my friends are such blockheads," he said.

"No problem," I said. "Mine are too."

Alex lived in Canton, one town over from Avon, in a new million-dollar development built a few yards shy of our exclusive Republican town line, sadly for him. That, he said, put him smack-dab in enemy camp, the economically depressed, Democratic-leaning Canton High School.

"I wish I lived in your town," he muttered to me, meaning his poorer friends were born and bred without the ability to pull themselves up by even the tiniest of boot-straps. The more he talked, the more I was sure Alex was the kind of guy who'd deregulate seal clubbing and repeal *Roe v. Wade*. And yet, he had such good hair, and was so hell-bent on being nice to me. Suddenly my principles didn't bother me so much. I gave him my phone number and he called the next day for a date.

As it turned out, Alex loved driving to my side of the tracks almost as much as I loved driving away from it. And in his Jeep, no less. He had a *Jeep*. A Jeep with no doors, no top, just a bare roll bar and a stripped-down dash.

"It's just a junk car," he said.

But the only junk car I'd ever been in that had its own door in a three-car garage.

After school, when he sailed into the roundabout in front of my high school and cut to a stop before me, it was as if a red carpet had unrolled at my feet. A flash of his sea-green eyes, his hairy knee against the tall gearshift, broad shoulders filling out a striped polo.

Are you getting this, people? I looked around to see if anyone else was sucking in their breath. A handful of no-bodies sat on the brick wall outside the school, waiting for their rides, squinting in the sun.

See? I gloated, taking a step toward my destiny. *In other towns, people like me.*

I took my place in the passenger seat and wondered how long I could keep Alex from realizing I had no friends to wave good-bye to.

"Let's get out of here," I said hurriedly, and he peeled out. Suddenly, there was wind in my hair. Suddenly, I had a life. With stipulations.

At heart, Alex was a businessman. He shook Dad's hand

like a corporate interviewee. He had a slide presentation of his productivity and a statistical analysis of his on-time curfew performance. *Thank you for the opportunity to prove myself, sir.* He was up to snuff on chitchat about the state of affairs and the latest election.

"The problem with most people is laziness," he said, coaxing the incredulous nod from Dad in our marble foyer. "They want the government to do it for them."

"I like your dad," Alex said later, in the car, five minutes after meeting him. "Great guy. He's worked hard to get himself where he's at."

"Mm-hm," I said, longing to suck the side of Alex's tanned neck.

"C'mon, ya hippie!" he hollered, shattering my trance. "Move it, fuckpuppy!" He was punishing the horn at a little VW Bug with peace sign stickers and apparently very bad timing at the stoplight. Confrontation terrified me, especially when directed at hippies. It was extra super awkward too, because we had no doors and no roof, and I had only a cheap plastic purse to shield my identity. But when it was over, Mr. Polite returned, smiling and reaching over to hold my hand. I couldn't be mad at that. I gave him one quick flash of my loaded expression, which contained a punishing dose of disapproval and just a hint of perfume.

As we drove along, I waxed philosophical about how his anger management issues were probably just y'know, normal Republican behavior. I positioned my legs against the seat, so they did not spread at all, with my left hand carefully covering the dimples of cellulite. The trick seemed to work because on a free stretch of road, Alex leaned over for a kiss.

Oh, he wants me, I thought. Maybe the wind had fluffed my hair up or something! Maybe it was the nonjudgmental way I handled his road rage! Whatever it was, Alex likey. He swerved off the road, drove across the railroad tracks, into the thicket, and down a muddy ditch. I pretended to appreciate the scenery until he turned off the engine, and then we attacked each other. Wanting more, I crawled over to sit on Alex's lap, a position that skewed all things in my mind. True, I'd been here before, but I had my big-girl panties on now, and they were coming off straightaway. No illegal end zones, no skittering away like a lemming off the cliff. My left hand uprooted hunks of his neatly tucked polo shirt, while my right thrust down into the front of his shorts, yanking his hard dick like a gearshift. One word flashed in my mind like a giddy caution light: big. And I was ready to make out in a way that alarmed me, and probably him.

"Whoa, we gotta stop," he said. I was both disappointed and relieved that he'd volunteered to be the moral authority here. That was supposed to be my job.

"We gotta." His breath was shaky, his hair mussed where I'd been grabbing handfuls. "Before this goes . . . too far."

He pecked my lips and tucked his shirt back into place.

Ironically, Alex's virtue triggered the exact opposite reaction in me.

Did his balls really turn blue? I wondered as I moved back into my seat. A single thought came into sharp focus: blow job. I had to. I remembered what Mallory had told me on a long bus trip to a basketball game we would lose: *You can't let him get blue balls. You have to give a guy a bj, or he'll go looking for it somewhere else.* Couldn't let that happen. But what would God say? And my parents? Oh, the untold shock and horror. But they would never know.

And even if they did, at least it wasn't sex, like the kind everybody else was having. No, wait. Maybe it was worse. Whatever. They would never find out. Ever.

As I did exercises to loosen my jaw, Alex kept calling. Night after night, good hair day or bad, bases loaded or empty, he still wanted to hear my voice. It was a miracle. It really helped that we didn't go to the same school and that he didn't witness certain things, like the KICK ME note I'd found taped to the back of my sweater. I framed a photograph of us and set it on my bedside table. Whenever I stared at it, my heart melted. How could he be so nice? Why did I look so pretty next to him? Maybe it was love. Or happiness. Or a ticking time bomb. I had to do something.

A few Friday nights later, we took a blanket and walked across the street from his parents' castle to another McMansion still under construction. The moon shone through empty window frames, making bright rectangles on the particle board. We wandered in and out of the maze of beams, making small talk.

"Nice view," he said, looking out.

"I know," I echoed, staring at the way his hair swept up off his forehead, at the hard, broad span of his shoulders. Within minutes, I was clawing at his upper leg. He kissed me back, dipping his hands cautiously in and out of my clothes, humming a little when I grazed his rock-hard crotch. He threw the blanket on the dusty floor, and I threw off my shirt like an old hat.

It's okay, I told Jesus as I undressed Alex. *We talk for hours.* I jangled the belt at his waist and he kicked off his shorts. *He pulls out my chair and opens my door and makes really sweet mix tapes for me.* I slid the elastic down his hips and over his knees. *He even goes to church, albeit a Lutheran one.* I took him in both hands, giddy with excitement. *And he's so freakin' BIG.*

I wanted to roll like a dog in his cologne, rev his erection like a gas pedal, spin his dials with my fingertips, make him squeeze me tighter until I felt his devotion, or at least a highly acceptable carbon copy. And although I was pretty sure I was about to shortchange the man I'd marry of first fellatio, I was also pretty sure it would be worth it. And if it wasn't, I was pretty sure I didn't care.

On the drive over here I'd been listening to a song on the radio. "How can something so right," it went, "be so wrong?" The short answer was, if it didn't penetrate the vagina, then technically it was not wrong. The longer answer was, sometimes getting felt under your panties is so hot it's almost pure. Pure and right and you can cry about the rest later.

When Alex's hands started doing that, I fell in step with a completely new signal, one not previously emitted by the heavenly hosts. *Hello,* I said to the rest of my life and reached down to chuck my underwear across the floor. *More, please.* I had scrubbed my parts for days, just in case this might happen. I wasn't planning for it or anything. But, I thought, just in case his face might happen to, you know, accidentally graze my naked naughty bits, I wanted to be spring fresh.

Alex peeked down at my crotch, then began to kiss southward. I held my breath. *Here it comes.* Down lower, lower still. *Hello lover!* Then: full stop. Up and over, repeat. Down my waist, up and over, up my thigh again. I awaited approval but instead got cold feet, or worse, maybe panic.

The caution flag was definitely waving. He wasn't teasing me, he was stalling. This was terror, not technique. He was scared of kissing me down there. Was I too hairy? Too freaky looking? But *ugh,* these were anatomically unavoidable problems!

I pretended to act casual as he rolled over onto his elbow for a pit stop, like he'd thought of a better idea. *Should I apologize?* I wondered. *I'm sorry for having a vagina.* But his hand was still touching me, testing to see if it was okay, suddenly making up for everything with a deep stroke between my legs, folding all my years of careful excuses like a house of cards. *Buh-bye, third base. So long.* Not only was I giving way but I was arching to get more, to completely dissolve his body in mine. For a few minutes, there was nothing else in the entire universe except his hands and his beautiful sea-green eyes, watching me shudder with pleasure.

Then I started to worry.

All of his deep-sea drilling was a means to an orgasmic end, I knew, but what that end was, or how to get there, I knew not. But how could I possibly stop to explain that? The minutes passed, too many minutes of Alex trying to get the genie out of the lamp, solve the Rubik's Cube, fill in all the bubbles of my anatomical SAT. He was probably getting bored. Maybe we should stop and switch. When do we stop? When do we call in the pinch hitter? I didn't want it to stop, but the idea of Alex suffering from carpal tunnel was unbearable. I wasn't supposed to just lie here. *Quick, what would the perfect girlfriend do in this situation?* She would end it on the right note. She would please everybody. She would attempt a high-pitched sigh, maybe a meaningful hum—something that says "that's a wrap" without discouraging future attempts. And so, the moment of truth prepared for its hearty smackdown.

"*Ahhhh,*" I purred.

A bit unsavory, but effective.

"Did you?" he asked.

"Yeah," I lied.

Relieved, we turned to the less complicated arena of his body: this, the plainest view I'd ever had of a hard, naked man. I dusted off my deceit and pinned him against the floor.

"What're you doing?" He grinned, knowing.

"Your turn," I said.

I was ready to make it last forever.

I indulged in my face-to-dick introduction, sliding my palm over the silky shaft, liking how he shivered when I cupped the tip in my hand. I kissed his stomach, drawing lower and drooling, licking up and down. How, I marveled, could a girl fit that sucker in her mouth, let alone anywhere else? But luckily, another side of my personality was poised to emerge: Xena the Mighty Cock Lover. *You have the gift,* said the narrator. *Take him. Now!* I grabbed the thing and yanked it sideways like a dagger, making him breathe harder.

"Alex," I warned, trying to think of some fitting last words. *It's been fun not being a slut . . . I'd like to thank God . . . and my parents . . .*

Then I devoured him, sucked him like candy, battered my gag reflex, pulled until my jaw ached, saliva running down into my fist.

His strong, lean body trembled, and he let out a funny-sounding cry that filled me with giggly prowess. I stamped down the retch and swallowed what came up like it was no big deal, trying not to taste whatever the hell that was. *Semen,* explained my textbook. That is *ejaculate.* That is *nasty,* I thought. It had the consistency of snot and the flavor of bile. I kept hearing Mallory's voice: *swallow it! You have to swallow. Guys like girls who swallow better.* I obeyed and wiped my mouth with the back of my forearm, trying not to let him see my whole body convulse with the aftershock retch.

With his lust exhausted and mine still crackling, we curled up together nude, my legs wrapped around his side. But as the high receded, the guilt crept in. I became aware that somewhere, God, the future, and mankind still existed. Soon I would return to my parents' house fully dressed, acting like nothing had happened. *Yeah, Mom, we just went for a walk and got some, uh, some ice cream?* I was still a virgin, just a third-and-a-half-base virgin. Future husband would be okay with that, I guess. It was love, after all. Possibly love. A lot like love. And if anyone was supposed to understand the power of love, it was Jesus Christ.

As a bonus, I didn't have to worry about Alex pressuring me to have sex. He would never go that far, on account of his Republicanesque drive to always first consider my dad's wishes. So that was great. The making out—that was great too. But the routine began to suck. Literally. I was always sucking on him, right after faking it. My professionally canned reaction was my secret shame, but I decided that was the price of keeping the blue out of his balls and his phone calls coming, and ensuring that punch-drunk gaze would be forever mine.

Although I didn't know how to climax, I never gave up the hope that if I preened obsessively enough I could help him get over his fear of licking and kissing my female parts. Before seeing him, I locked myself in the bathroom for hours with boxes of waxing strips, loofahs and scented soaps. Though shaving the whole thing bare never occurred to me, I scrubbed, inspected, groomed, and powdered until my crotch was cryogenically preserved. I tried a sample, pretending I was him, touching then tasting myself. Seemed okay. A little powdery, but so were doughnuts, and everyone liked doughnuts.

Still, when viewed in a hand mirror the vagina was scary and strange, even to me, its owner. I didn't look at it too long, for fear it would bite me and I'd get demoralized. One could understand what guys were up against.

But the next time we ended up in the back of his dad's car, pants unzipped, it was the same thing. He made a move like he was going to go down on me—head lowering into my lap, slowing, stalling—then thinking better of the whole thing.

"I can't," he said, not explaining, resorting to his hands while I covered my honesty with pleasing sighs.

I was such a fake.

He dropped me off at home and I watched through the storm door as his taillights receded up and over the hill, stealing my air as they went. I dragged myself up the stairs and cried, churning with doubt. A half hour later the phone, as always, would ring. Alex: saving me. Maybe he knew but couldn't exactly talk about it. Neither could I.

"Hey!" I said, wiping tears, careful to keep my voice in the acceptable range of Never Happier.

"Hi. Just making sure you're all right."

"Yeah, I'm good! How are you?"

"Good."

"That's good, that's good," I blathered. "Good, I'm glad."

"I just want you to be happy," he said. "That's all that matters."

"Aw," I said, and fell back on my bed in a puddle, crying again. I reached out to touch the picture frame, shifting it so I could stare at his smile. I couldn't wait to see him again and do the whole stupid thing over again.

The next time he showed up at my house, he dismounted his Jeep—looking like Lancelot as usual—and presented me with a CD player and some headphones.

"What's this?"

"Just listen," he said. "You gotta hear it."

I climbed into the passenger seat of the parked Jeep, listening to the music as if my life depended on it. It was "Why" by Annie Lennox. I spot-memorized every lyric, every lovely cadence, wondering if the song had anything to do with the way he felt about me. You could never tell, and Alex didn't say. He just stood apart, leaning over the back tire, dying for someone to read his mind. I understood the need. It was the same as me pointing my Walkman at heaven, waiting for God's cryptic FM message for my life.

I pondered "Why" for weeks, never sure what the last line meant. Was it, *you don't know what I fear*? Or was it, *you don't know what I feel*? Two entirely different endings to our relationship, two completely different diagnoses.

Was trouble brewing? Was a breakup on the horizon?

I thought about giving him my favorite song, Tori Amos's "Silent All These Years." But her soothing growl of lucid and fiery female rage was too out of character for the version of me that he knew. Too dark, too dangerously negative. It was safer to focus only on the things that he liked.

Like Rush Limbaugh.

I started tuning in to Rush at noon because I believed he was the one man who understood Alex better than I did. And I wanted Alex to feel like we were on the same wavelength, even if it meant partially destroying my own frequency.

During lunch period I slipped out behind the school to my parked station wagon, sandwich in tow. I strained forward, listening hard through the AM radio buzz. Rush was like a fire-and-brimstone preacher, only he offered no chance at redemption for bleeding hearts like me. Every three sentences or so I got punched in the gut. But hey, a daily political smackdown was definitely better than eating lunch in a locked stall in the girls' locker room.

"Liberals!" Rush barked. "Liberals and feminazis!"

Sometimes I couldn't even chew. That was *me* he was talking about. *Liberal,* almost synonymous with *pedophile.* I now understood how dangerous it would be for Alex to discover my socialist-leaning, progressively feminist default settings. Getting punished for them helped. It gave my life purpose, brought us sooo much closer. And compared to the prospect of losing his love, the live burial of my budding identity was something I could learn to live with.

With my right-wing radio routine in full swing, and a subscription to *National Review* complete, I dove headfirst into library books on how to love, how to be more lovable, more loving, how to get love, how to keep it. There I was, standing in line to check out with my stack of relationship books, when I saw *The Beauty Myth* by Naomi Wolf on the New Releases shelf. Its subtitle glowed. I had never read anything like it before: *How Images of Beauty Are Used Against Women.*

I left the line, put down my other books and grabbed it, thumbing through the pages until I came to rest on a chapter titled "Sex." It began:

> **Religious guilt represses women's sexuality.**
>
> Technically, the female sexual organs are what the older religions feared as "the insatiable cunt." Capable of multiple orgasm, continual orgasm, a sharp and breathtaking clitoral orgasm, an orgasm seemingly centered in the vagina that is emotionally overwhelming, orgasm from having the breasts stroked, and of endless variations of all those responses combined, women's capacity for genital pleasure is theoretically inexhaustible.
>
> But women's prodigious sexual capacity is not being reflected in their current sexual experience.

I looked around wildly, wanting to yell at someone, the librarians maybe. *You guys hearing this?* It was so nasty. It was so shocking. It was the best news in years.

> Is "beauty" really sex? Does a woman's sexuality correspond to what she looks like? Does she have the right to sexual pleasure and self-esteem because she's a person, or must she earn that right through "beauty"?

I stood nailed to the ground, squirming a little, as if a finger had been placed directly on the pulse of my own pain, on a cold seed at my core, unable to grow. I turned the book over to stare down the author's photo. *Who are you and what planet do you come from?* I had to take her home, claim her as my own, and inspect her further.

So I checked out *The Beauty Myth*, along with a dozen other books, including a tell-all about what men secretly wanted women to do to their penises. Soon I would be supped full on the best possible way to behave in a million different scenarios, and also a growing sense that I was doing them for all the wrong reasons.

Later that week, I sat on a bank of grass at Alex's high school baseball game. I didn't really care if his team lost. I didn't really care about baseball. I did, however, care a lot about a new technique called the *scrotal tug*. When I saw him in his tight gray pants, peeling a batting glove off his strong, tan hand, I couldn't wait to try it on him.

"Good game, guys!" he hollered to his team in his road rage octave. "We'll get 'em next time!"

Ironically, although he was captain, the other players seemed to brush him off. I knew exactly what their telltale silence meant. It meant *shut the hell up*. They didn't like him. It was his senior year, but he was still just a new kid here. If he cared how it looked to be panned, he didn't let it show. He strode on over to me, smiling.

"Hi," he said. "Sorry you had to come to such a shitty game."

My hair coiffed to extremes, my mind brimming with wildly opposing dogma, all I could do was proudly plant a kiss on him, then watch him saunter back to his team. No one talked to him. He packed his equipment in silence, and I marveled at the rejection. Apparently I wasn't the only one who needed a better life.

No wonder he likes me, I realized. He really had no other options.

• • •

A couple months later, Alex had to leave. College for him, the end of life support for me. I'd always known it was coming but hadn't known what it meant, at least not until I kissed him good-bye at his front door for the last time.

I walked away toward my car, waving the wave of an inmate returning to prison. A few more steps, one last wave—slightly less convincing but still in one piece—got in my car and turned the key. The air drained out and the suffocating upholstery sealed me in, the hermetic windshield mashing my face flat against my empty future. I looked back at Alex one last time, just as his head disappeared and his front door sealed flush with the frame. Our ribbon pulled thin and snapped, and I fell apart.

My foot was on the gas pedal, but I was sobbing so hard I could barely make out the dashboard or the road in my headlights, all of it expecting me to drive home, to accept that I had fallen in love, but the only thing left to prove it now was a picture frame. The life I'd tried so hard to escape would now be resumed in progress. Only minus Rush Limbaugh. Well, at least that was one bright spot. I'd always pine for Alex, but it was time for Rush and his oppressive jowls to evaporate, *poof,* back into the pall of AM static from whence they came, never to return. Thank God.

At long last, my senior year had arrived, and I marked the occasion by moping. In art class, I stared at our teacher as he sat at his desk, dabbling at a charcoal sketch of Ashley. Year after year, season after season, Avon's love for her had only grown stronger. Now even the art teacher wanted to immortalize her on canvas, so he could put her lovely mug in the glass art showcase in the main hall, deeming her fit for mass consumption. As if she needed one more fucking reason to feel good about herself.

While Ashley sat in a chair at the front of the room holding her profile in place, the rest of us were assigned to make our own mediocre copies of classic works of art.

We huddled around the bin of prints like hobos at a trash barrel, trying to grab a scrap. I pulled out *The Birth of Venus* and sat down at the long paint-stained table to consider the goddess and the blissfully entangled cherubim hovering over her head. I looked around at the other students, one badly copying a Michelangelo, another yakking on about chemistry homework while attempting to pencil his Van Gogh. At the front of the room, the teacher, the only talented artist among us, continued to lose himself in the masterpiece that was Ashley. He looked at her the same way Alex had looked at me when I was naked.

I rolled my eyes and rattled a dirty can of used and broken colored pencils, clapping it down hard on the desk. A few people looked up, but no one in this zip code would ever see me.

The class before this had been choir rehearsal, where three other girls and I had taken turns singing a solo from "Panis Angelicus." As sopranos, the others had no trouble stuffing the rafters with operatic wadge. But when my turn came, I'd done the only thing a mediocre alto could do: imitate Mariah Carey on the verge of a mental breakdown.

At least I had soul, I consoled myself as they snickered.

Outside the art room, a cluster of excited girls in their field hockey skirts passed in the hallway, flaunting the uniform of the chosen few. A headstone of jealousy rose up in my chest, familiar and cold.

There was no way I was going to churn out yet another half-assed second-rate version of someone else's muse, or spend the rest of the semester passing Ashley's self-portrait in the hallway. Not this time. I needed some kind of rebuttal. Some kind of spotlight. Something I could call my own.

I squirted some paint on my palette and began to obsess over dabs of acrylic, hunting for the magic combination that would give me the hue of Alex's eyes, the folds of his striped cotton shirt, the color of his summer skin. I pulled out my dog-eared photograph of him standing beside the Jeep, the canopy of the lush summer forest rising up behind him, golden afternoon luster on everything. Out the art room window, nothing but cold, bare branches.

I pressed Play on my Walkman, so I could listen to Peter Gabriel's "Blood of Eden" over and over. Never once in my entire school career had I ever dared to skip class or play hooky. As a good girl, I preferred escaping like this, by going out of body via prerecorded music. Up through the roof I went, into a better place, into a magical past where I got to mentally airbrush all the facts. Instead of white and dorky, I'd be black and dreadlocked and powerful, covered in tribal paint, flying high above Avon Mountain, wrapping Alex in my arms, carrying him spellbound into bliss.

The art teacher looked in over my shoulder and grunted.

"You need to fix that," he said, tapping the skewed angle on her exposed breast, the dark nipple. For a man who loved sketching prom queens, he had a disturbing knack for getting naked boobs just right. Then he added a dab of gray to the craters on the moon.

"Wow," I marveled, repeating the brushstroke.

"This was due two weeks ago," he said, frowning and stroking his thick red beard. "But still, it's wicked."

"It's Alex," I corrected. "And me."

The art teacher hung it in the showcase in the hall, right next to the charcoal of Ashley, who while always pretty, looked a little boring next to my pair of flying seminude interracial lovers. As I paused in the hallway, taking in my masterpiece, someone stopped beside me. Some kid I hardly talked to.

"That is awesome," he said, like he meant it. "That's Avon Mountain, right?"

"Yeah! It is!" I said.

"Hey, is that your tit right there?" he asked, pointing.

"Um, you mean that *black girl*?" I replied, squirming.

"Totally phallic, that little tower in the background."

"Hmm," I sighed, disappointed that I'd somehow missed this tiny, subconsciously painted erection. I should've made it bigger.

While the judges at the local art show deemed my phili-ophallic painting worthy of honorable mention, Alex came home for Christmas.

"I have a basketball game," I told him on the phone, jumping out of my skin, fixing my ponytail. "I have to be there at six."

"I can take you," he offered. "Maybe we can grab a bite?"

I hit the ceiling, running up and down the upstairs hall-ways of our house, screaming about Alex picking me up.

He looked as well dressed and hot as ever, but even more achingly above my pay grade. He wore a long camel trench coat that made him look like a man. Like Zeus. It hurt a little to look at him.

His family had sold the Jeep, so we drove around in his mom's sedan, talked about college, fraternities, hazing, blah blah blah. I waited patiently for the only part that mattered: Did he still love me?

"I thought about you," he said. He thought about me? It was enough. I leaned over to kiss him, seize him; I would have bought him if I could have. I didn't want to know any more about the stupid details. *Just let me own you,* my kisses begged. *Just for five minutes, my head bobbing in your lap. Please.*

It was already dark when he dropped me off at my game. I hopped out in my basketball uniform and waved, crunching over the icy snow into the doors of the gym. Warm-ups had already started. Mallory, my fellow benchie and purveyor of sex tips, dribbled over to sum me up.

"Where you been?" she asked. "You're late."

"Alex dropped me off."

"Ooo, Alex." She grinned, zooming in. "He's back, huh."

"Yeah, he's back," I sighed.

"What's that all over your face?"

I shied back. "What?"

"Oh my God," she giggled. "What have you been eating? It's all over."

"Nothing," I said, blushing, touching my chin and cheek and feeling something. I ducked into the locker room.

"Hold up," she said, smiling. "I know what that is. Hold up."

I ran to the mirror. She followed.

"I know what that is," she sang. "Ha-ha." There was a white film all over my face, dried to a crust. I turned on the faucet and dabbed with an industrial paper towel, stupid, stupid, *stupid.*

"You've been sucking dick."

"What? No!" I lied, my pride swirling down into the sink, wondering what it was I got out of Alex other than a whole lot of nothing. Maybe he had used me, but why had I begged him to? I'd painted him into my Botticelli, and he'd sent me off to play second string, with the mark of the Beast all over my face.

12 | The Second Coming, Starring Sonny Crockett

> "Thou madest to thyself images of men,
> and didst commit whoredom with them."
>
> —EZEKIEL 16:17

Growing up, I always had a Harlequin Romance stashed somewhere. But in those books, or at least in the sorry-ass ones I ended up with, it was always the man who had the "climax," never the woman. Or maybe she did, maybe it just got lost amid all the bodice ripping and face slapping.

The only truly and bluntly dirty book I'd ever gotten my mitts on was *Crazy Ladies,* a thick paperback I'd dug out of the bottom of the local library's dollar box. On the cover were four outdated photographs of seminaked women with '70s hairdos and ample breasts, and stories that would indelibly brand my temporal lobe. For God's sake, Pursettes stuck in vaginas? What the ... midgets with clap toes? Nipple holes cut in bras and clits getting rubbed raw? It was a high-speed train wreck of Naughty, and I practically photocopied each word with my eyeballs. I understood only about one-fifth of what was going on, but I was still devastated when Mom found the book hidden under my bed and confiscated it. I was left to assume that a clit was, I don't know, maybe a slang word for vagina. Or a French birth defect.

Thankfully, right before my eighteenth birthday, Kate came home from college and helped me cut through the cloud of romantic smog. She, the unwitting activator on the wilting Jheri curl of my well-read but poorly understood sex life.

She was unpacking her bags and sorting stuff in her room, and I was rifling through a box of her pictures from parties, formals, and dates. Life far, far away from our idyllic town looked much, much more ideal.

Things at Avon High School had been just as hard for Kate, socially speaking. We, the awkward and self-conscious sisters whose only claim to fame was our inexplicable blood relation to a member of homecoming royalty, our older brother. But the biggest difference between me and Kate was that she at least had friends. Wherever she went, she made tons and tons of friends. I, however, preferred to hide in a cave and chew on the carcass of whatever guy I had temporarily dragged away to dry hump.

"Who's this?" I asked, holding up a photo taken at some party. Kate snickered.

"Oh, my gosh."

"What?"

"Those are my hall mates. We get so crazy."

"Like how?"

"I don't know, jumping in the fountain. Throwing people

in the lake." Then she lowered her voice, though no one was in earshot. "Masturbating in the hot tub."

"Jumping in the—" I interrupted, the photo going limp in my hand. "Wait, what?"

"Yeah." She laughed.

"The hot tub. The hot tub?"

"Yup. On the jets."

"The jets," I echoed.

"My friend does it all the time. When she takes a bath, we all know what she's doing. She takes for-*ever.*"

"Ha!" I blurted out, not really laughing. "Ha!"

"One night, she got a bunch of us to do it together. We were kinda drunk."

"Too funny," I mumbled, dazed.

It wasn't like I didn't know stuff. I had stayed at the library for four hours one afternoon so I could read the entire *Kinsey Report* cover to cover. I had memorized every sexual statistic ever printed since the dawn of time. Oh, I understood about masturbation all right. I just didn't *get it.* At all.

"How do you do that exactly?" I asked.

My sister looked up from sorting her jewelry, a touch of dread in her eyes. But she forged ahead.

"Well, you can like, use a washcloth."

"A washcloth."

"Yeah," she said, "take it in the shower. That's what I did. You feel around, and . . . you know . . . *practice.*"

Practice, I thought. *Practice.* I was good at practicing. I practiced everything.

"It takes longer for girls."

"But what happens?"

Sis looked at me. "What happens is, you have an orgasm." She explained. "And trust me, it's worth it."

Her voice echoed for miles, across the dimensions of sight and sound. *Orgasm . . . Orgasm . . . Orgasm.*

I found out straightaway that standing in the shower with a limp rag did nothing for me but make me very clean. I lay in bed and put a hand on myself but all I could think about was rearranging the furniture in my bedroom. I rolled onto my side, wondering how long the Greenpeace poster on my wall had been hanging crooked, and should I get up to fix it. Seriously, why hadn't I ever fixed that?

Orgasm, my brain reminded me. *Orgasm.*

Back to the drawing board. I picked up my hand mirror and my latest replacement for low-grade romance: an anatomy book on female sexuality. I took them both into the bathroom and locked the door. I wasn't here to play. I wasn't here to shave or powder or make it pretty, or to spread the folds and cower in fear. I was going to diagram and identify my parts. I was going to document them, rope them into submission, and read to them from the Holy Book of Vagina.

I opened to the graphically enlarged, frontally positioned, leg-splayed diagram of the Female Genitalia, complete with stylish pubes. Using a tube of toothpaste to weigh down the pages, I squatted over the mirror and stared. First at me, then the diagram. Then me. Then the diagram.

Vagina. *Check.*

But oh my God, it was so much like guts. Guts on the outside. Pink tissue of all strange varieties and shapes, some smooth, some chewed, like overlapping pink petals, or pink-gummed fangs, depending on how you looked at it. Multiple points of entry into the dark abyss of my internal organs. Breathe. Keep going.

Urethra. *Check*.

Clitoris. *Holy crap*. I had those two completely confused. Wait. Clit-o-ris? Oh. Clit. *Oh! Clit!* All hidden under that tubey skin thing. I'd always wondered. *Nerve bundles, stimulation*. Behold, the "special place." Behold, the orgasm button! Dammit, why didn't they bother to mention that in health? That would've been kinda freaking helpful.

I stared for a while at the list of icky names, vulva and labia and mons pubis, as if scientists had gone out of their way to make women's parts sound like organ meat cold cuts. Why not something more inviting, like a LeTigre or a Bunny?

I pulled back the sheath and poked gently at my clit-o-ris. Ouch. No way. That? That was the pleasure center? Couldn't be. It was like jabbing the point of an ice cube into a sensitive tooth. What a joke. How would that ever feel good? You needed a guy to, like, jump-start everything. And who knew when one of those was coming along and whether or not he read anatomy books. Mystery unsolved.

Crap.

So I went back to doing what I did best: praying and baking. Cookies, of course.

One Friday night, while my fourth batch browned, I sat on the couch with one oven mitt still on, searching for something on TV to watch. I flipped past commercials and sitcoms and local news, and finally came to rest on the most interesting thing I could find: a pair of brown boobs in a white bikini bouncing to a mechanized steel drumbeat. It was only a *Miami Vice* rerun, but for a Tubbs-'n'-Crockett virgin like me, it was like being touched for the first time. God bless syndication.

Miami Vice, I soon discovered, was a nonstop music

video in a minor key, with only occasional breaks for dialogue where someone inevitably said, "It's going down tonight!" Only unlike MTV, it was all men: men, men, and more men, all of them troubled, tan, and windblown. And apparently going down! But none of them were more troubled or tan than Mr. Pissed-off in Pink, Sonny Crockett. Within three seconds, I was obsessed with him. I needed a poster or an injection or a bite guard or *something*. How could I not be in agony? He put on such a tough act, and yet according to the music, he was secretly sad and lonesome, torn by his failures! But he was so sweet sometimes, and playful too. So unbelievably, searingly, ridiculously yummy. He filled my panties with longing.

Plus, when he wasn't loading his gun, he was strapping it onto his bare skin, cocking it, pulling it back, and snapping it into play, sliding it down his pants so the barrel rested just above his ass. Then he rolled shirtless out of some girl's bed. I stared at the actress as she pulled the sheet up over her tits and grinned at him. Oh, my goodness, he was so much prettier than her. And yet—he still slept with her and her terrible overpermed bangs! There was hope! Holy crapballs, that could be *me*!

He kissed her and fastened on his shoulder holster and his leg holster—igniting a myriad of subconscious bondage fantasies—then slipped on his white linen jacket and off he went to kick ass and take names in Italian slippers, his stomach hard and his balls empty.

The commercials came on and I snapped to. There was smoke coming out of the oven, my cookies were black, and my eyes were the exact same shape as Don Johnson's supple ass. I had but one directive: to see him seminaked as many times in a row as was humanly possible. The only way to do this, in 1993, was to transform our clunky VCR into a love-scene-splicing machine. A video collage that I would fondly name "All Things Crockett."

It wasn't easy to edit back then. I had to rewind and forward endlessly, rewind and forward, then rewind, then forward just a touch, then rewind again, then get pissed off and forward two touches, then pause right where I left off, and then wait by the TV until any hint of a love scene was about to start, then press Record, then stop when they switched to the drug bust, or a commercial, then record again when they went back to the bedroom. It was highly exhausting and had to be completed while Mom was walking back and forth between her office and the kitchen, without giving her any indication that I had traded homemade soft-batch cookies for homemade soft-core porn.

Finally, once I'd gotten a week's worth of Crockett on tape, I would lie on the couch on Friday night, watching Dullfest, ABC's movie of the week, waiting until Mom and Dad were safely upstairs in bed. When all walking noises in the house ceased, I got up and pushed in my VHS tape, snuggled under the blanket, and glued my thumb to the buttons on the remote as if they were written in Braille.

First static, then the bass boomed and the surf rolled. Phil Collins crooned. Crockett sat silhouetted in the sunset, his long, massive Stinger boat idling.

I immediately imagined him naked and my eyes rolled back into my head. Oh, what his body could do to a woman. I had no idea really, but he knew. I wanted him to show me. But no, he didn't have time for that right now! He wasn't some womanizer; he had to reload his gun, rev his '72 Ferrari Daytona Spyder into third gear, and rocket through the dust along a lonesome highway. Behind him, the warehouse exploded and his glistening tan grew deeper, the whites of his fingernails gleaming, secretly made for untying the bikini strings over a woman's naked butt cheeks. And also pulling the trigger to protect them. The synthesizer began to brood over the chrome rims of his spinning wheels.

Then my tape warbled a bit, crinkling inside the VCR, then straightened out and swan-dived right into some made-for-TV sex. His strappy gun holster dropped on the dock—*thud*—and the white jacket too—*whoosh*—revealing a sleeveless baby blue T. Something only a true man would wear. He wasn't incredibly built or anything. He was just incredibly *male*. There was one vein running along a biceps. The camera zeroed in on his light eyes.

Holy Crockett, I whispered. *There should be a law.*

Unable to take any more, I slid my hand into my pajamas over the correct locale. It was only an experiment. What would happen if you combined visual pleasure with knowledge of physiology? Hypothesis one: shame and humiliation. Hypothesis two: an answered prayer.

The electric guitar whined and Sonny pressed down on top of some chick. They shot the scene in brief, FCC-approved stages of undress, all of it masked in frustrating shadows and choreography, panning away before they showed his hands going any lower. I played it back six, seven, ten times so as not to miss his fingertips, his eyes, his teeth. I wondered about the cameraman filming them. I wondered what it felt like to be that woman. They must've been so embarrassed—and so turned on. So lucky! As consolation, I applied the desired pressure between my legs, gave a few test repetitions. With my free hand I hit Play, Rewind, Play, Rewind. I lay back and watched Sonny's head moving down, presumably to suck her nipples offscreen.

Pause. *This is what his face looks like,* I told myself, *right before he devours a pair of tits.* Then in the next shot he kissed her belly lower and lower and lower. Just before he dipped offscreen, I hit Pause. *This is what his face looks like,* I shifted out of my pajama pants, *right before he devours a woman's clit-o-ris.*

I stopped to catch my breath, amazed. This little button on my body, a secret escape hatch to any sex life I wanted.

The next scene was dialogue and plot, the drug cartel this and Cortez that, blah blah blah, so I turned on my side away from the screen and continued to play the love scene in my mind, everything the censors would not allow: his hands kneading her sexy thighs, peering between her legs before he kissed her and licked her naked body. My hand moved faster. He was naked now, his straps and guns and armor gone, weakened and tender as his hard hot body jammed all the way inside her.

Houston, we are breaking up. We are breaking up, do you copy?

After all, he didn't want to hurt her, but he had to get his fill, ramming her hard right there, right there, over and over.

A wave much bigger than my body was rising up, I could feel it coming. Just had to keep moving my hand or I would drop this delicate thread, this kite string lifting me upward, the gentle but insistent pull of a single helium balloon. The pleasure and agony swelled, twisting between my fingers tighter and sweeter until, suddenly, I caught a flash of how he looked letting go of his cool, how good he was at fucking, how everyone secretly longed to watch him doing it to her but they couldn't. Only she could watch. Only me.

Then I came. I exploded into ecstasy, fluttered weightless, sighing, the prize of his sex delivered on a silver platter, smoothed out and throbbing in my lap. There was nothing I could do but lie there trying to hold it a few seconds longer, the tide gently receding, leaving me pulsing and hot between my legs. I breathed it out and flopped my hand over my eyes, still clutching the remote, tears rolling softly back into my hair.

The next day I ejected my *Miami Vice* tape from the player and wrote DO NOT ERASE on the label, staring through the plastic window at the reel of magic. Then again on the cover: DO. NOT. ERASE. I pushed it back on the shelf between all the other wholesome family home movies—my brother's graduation, my sister's National Honor Society banquet—but it still glimmered like a golden calf. Like the south Florida sun on Jan Hammer's synthesizer.

Again tonight? Sonny asked, his two-day stubble promising even rougher treatment.

Yes, I answered. *Sex. Again. Tonight.*

Oh, it was going to be a long, hot summer. A long, hot summer at last.

13 | Soul Mates Can Be Annoying

"... and thy desire shall be to thy husband,
and he shall rule over thee."

—GENESIS 3:16

I spent my first day of college vomiting in the sink with the shades drawn.

The week after that, I moved into the boys' dorm to pledge my life and virginity to Justin, an eighteen-year-old spiritual baba. And by baba I mean my adult pacifier. Back in high school, my version of a hot Saturday night was sweating beside the oven in house slippers. But now I had finally arrived, swilling Malibu rum straight from the bottle by ten, walking to the frat house in a pod of females I'd just met, united in skank.

I'd never had liquor before. My brush with the dark side consisted of half a bottle of Bartles & Jaymes, and that was over a year ago. So I didn't understand why all my new BFFs sipped their Styrofoam cups so cautiously.

"Um, don't you think you ought to take it easy?" someone asked me.

"I don't feel anything." I shrugged, taking another gulp. "Stuff is weak."

I did feel something, however. The determination to entertain!

We walked along the wire fence that cordoned off the quad, and I tried to perch on it like a pigeon. I lost my balance and landed with my legs tangled above my head, coconut rum splashed across my suddenly exposed tit, you know, hilarious. It never occurred to me that I was the protagonist at the beginning of a cautionary tale. The other girls asked me if I was okay, oh-my-God-ing about how wasted I was.

"I am not," I said, thinking, *Yay, they like me! This is me! Going to a par-tay!*

"Hi!" I screamed at a passing car. "Hey, baby!"

It was an amazing sensation, bonding with females via group drunkenness. We were the sun in a heliocentric universe that emerged only at night. Bars and boys orbited our every whim. Gulping down more of the Brave New Me, I presented myself on the steps of the brotherhood. I was highly disoriented and with self-esteem roughly the size of my halter top.

"You!" I yelled. "Haul me up to the gang-rape loft for inspection."

The band was so loud no one could hear my clever puns. I stumbled upward into the wafting perfume of beer and urine, took a hit off a freshly lit cigarette and inhaled deep. The wooden Greek letters nailed over the Confederate flag tilted and hummed. A wave of light-headedness had me spinning so fast I could not feel my face. I slapped myself on the cheek—hard. Still not there. Again. I could, however, feel the bile rising in my throat. Oh, no. The *spinning*. The accursed and unrelenting spinning.

"Be right there," I told no one. The girls had gone on ahead, oblivious of their shrinking ranks. "Just a second. I'm going to . . . check out the fence, m-kay?"

Alarmed, I crouched in the shadows by some bushes and heaved up everything that was not connected to my spine. To the moon above me I offered sincere apologies. *Please help me* (bleh) *oh hell* (bleh) *oh God help* (bleh). Several guys stumbling across me on their way to pee stopped to make chitchat. I tilted up my head, wiping the chunky dribbles of vomit off my chin.

"Yeah," I moaned to one guy, "Kappa Alpha rocks."

As the hours wore on, my puking did not abate. Like a farm animal, I merely moved a few paces to the left to find fresh grass to lie in. Some magnanimous junior ordered her boyfriend to carry me to his car and drive me to my dorm. To me, he was an angel in human form, stepping in to save what was left of God's lost sheep and her one remaining nine-inch platform shoe.

I apologized to this stranger, my grass-stained forehead leaving a blot on his cold car window. He carried me up four flights of stairs and left. I kept asking him his name.

"I wanna send you a fricking Hallmark," I said. "Sorry, I don't swear, I swear. I'm a Christian."

When I appeared in the doorway draped over the shoulder of a strange man, my new roommate sat up in bed. I could see her beady eyes peeking over her comforter as I passed out next to my bucket.

"I'm going to tell the RA," she huffed, slipping into her bathrobe.

"Okay," I said. "I'll be right here."

• • •

At the seventy-two-hours-away-from-home mark, still queasy from the mere sound of the word *coconut*, I met Justin, my mate for life whom I hoped to spend my life mating with. He was a dark Jewish kid with full lips and a jarhead haircut. His massive beige Timberlands were purposefully unlaced and immaculately clean.

"Check out the army guy," I whispered to the girl next to me at orientation.

"He's on the floor below me," she told me. "But he's not in the army. He's from Palm Beach."

Justin was actually a militant pacifist who spent every possible second working out or reading Taoist philosophy, sometimes at the same time. To him, carefully sculpted calves were the outward manifestation of a deep and thoughtful personality. We exchanged looks. He looked like a cocky muscle head, until he smiled. Then it was plain as day: he was self-conscious. Our mutual virgin radar locked in.

"I'm Justin," he said with this giddy, vulnerable smile.

"Hi," I said. "I saw you the other day. Your dorm is across from the DUC, right?"

"Yeah," he said, smiling huge.

"What's so funny?" I asked.

"No, nothing. I've just seen you around and . . . now here you are. I'm finally talking to you."

"Oh, wow," I said. "Yeah me too. Talking to you."

"People always think I'm Puerto Rican. The hair, I guess."

"Oh. Yeah, I can see that."

But the first thing I noticed about Justin was his body. The second thing I noticed was his hang-up about it. *Not a hang-up*, I corrected myself, *just a health nut*. There was a difference.

At our first lunch date, he wrapped his chicken tenders, well, *tenderly* in paper napkins and then balled his fist around them and squeezed. Set 1: tight, tighter, tightest, then rest and chew. It was a death blot for grease, he explained, and also an exercise to build the forearm!

"I'm trying to get cut," he said as he fisted them for three more sets, until they were devoid of all saturated fat, color, and shape. All this I watched, slightly uneasy, while eating mine as is and with extra sauce.

But the wedding bells didn't go off like fire alarms until Justin paused over his uneaten tenders, bowed his head, and pinched his eyes closed. Just two seconds was all it took.

"Oh, you *pray*?" I asked, wondering how to broach the topic. "Are you . . . *religious*?"

Justin chewed slowly, thoughtfully, as if he wanted to phrase his answer in the wisest way possible.

"I am . . . *spiritual*," he said finally.

"Oh!" I brightened. "Me too!"

"I'm Jewish, but I believe there is a seed of truth in all religions. That's what I seek. Truth."

"That is so neat!" I bubbled, falling over myself. "I like that!"

"The prayer is more for the animals. To thank them for their sacrifice."

"Oh, my gosh!" I said, trying to control my minicoronary. I nodded, squinting at him, showing him that I was in complete and calm solidarity with thanking all the chickens of the world before defiling them with honey mustard. Why hadn't I thought of that? I hoped my hair looked okay. I hoped I wasn't too pudgy. I hoped I was as spiritual as he was. Justin smiled back at me with a big white grin and warm brown eyes.

I looked down at my Chick-fil-A box and realized I had wolfed down all my food. Only a few blots of grease and some crumbs remained.

"Sorry," I said, for some reason. "I just totally pigged."

"I eat slowly," he explained, his patient smile unwavering. "It's important to chew the correct number of times to increase protein absorption and, um, reduce flatulence."

When we were done, he tucked the rest of his chicken back into its cardboard house and toted them home where he'd hoard them and no doubt abuse them again later. I had so much to learn.

Meanwhile, the buzz on the floor back at my dorm was all about upcoming sorority rush. Like coveted crystals on *Mighty Morphin Power Rangers,* there were sororities of nerds, sororities of sluts, and sororities of power—but which did I have to defeat? Eager to not repeat any mistakes of the past, I asked around until a consensus emerged: all roads led to the house of Tri Delt, the Thunderdome of the Blond Skinny Bitches. That was the bull's-eye to shoot for in order to achieve the life I'd always dreamed of.

"It's about who you know there," one of my hall mates fretted. "That's why you have to go to the parties. You have to meet them, you have to stand with the right people, get them to like you."

My panic grew. How could I possibly win a battle I had just spent ten years losing? "They dig into your records," she warned. "They call your old high school and find out who you were friends with."

"Seriously?" I said, almost laughing but not quite.

"Seriously!" she said. "If you were a loser or a dork, trust me, *they will find out.*"

I looked right at her and realized: she had no idea who I really was. Otherwise she wouldn't have said that. Which was good. And also really, really bad.

It was easier being with Justin. Being his love interest had instantly earned me a ready-made center stage spot in the middle of a tight-knit crew of homies. They definitely didn't care about my shitty high school status. I soaked up their admiring looks in the hallways of the Pit, their smelly, damp, all-male basement dorm, where the walls vibrated with Snoop and Rage Against the Machine.

The second best thing about Justin was his roommate, Joe. He'd gone to Justin's high school, and they'd come to college as a kind of package deal, representing opposite ends of the male spectrum. Joe was pale, tall, and physically softer; Justin short, dark, and hard. As native Palm Beachians, being cut and ripped were their primary obsessions, but they had very different approaches. While Justin walked all day on the balls of his feet to achieve leg tone, Joe hoarded the latest in soft-core steroids. While Justin blotted and blessed his salad, Joe's shelves contained equal parts corn chips and powdered performance drinks declared illegal by the FDA. They had names like Turbo Rip-up and Studulated Oxygen MegaMass, with complicated windows of ingestion. Like ¼ cup thirty minutes before working out, then two cups five minutes after, or else your quads would shrivel up like raisins.

It didn't matter that Justin had a tight budget and no car—we had Joe, who pulled up in a brand-new black Bronco with custom oversize wheels and a *Dukes of Hazzard* horn that blasted at window-shattering decibels.

When Justin got bored, he read *The Art of War.* When Joe got bored, he chucked CDs out of his sunroof, three or four at a time, while speeding down the highway. He convinced every guy who was shorter than him to help fill the RA's room with six feet of shaving cream and move the Pit's lounge furniture out into the parking lot.

At parties, Joe chugged gallon jugs of vodka and cranberry, while Justin sipped a Zima with me and got cuddly and weird, preaching to complete strangers about how young women needed to be treated with more respect. Meanwhile Joe slumped over the shoulder of an obliging frat ho and puked down her back.

He laughed. "I need a refill."

"You are so fucked up!" screamed his date, wiping off puke with a paper towel, her lit cigarette nearly catching Joe in the eye.

That could be me, I thought, both recoiling and admiring at the same time. There was an undeniable charm in being a total hobag. But I didn't tell Justin that. He was standing by my side, sadly shaking his head.

"So lost," he whispered.

"Yeah," I agreed. But the next day, I attended my first sorority rush meet 'n' greet.

A few of my female hall mates and I got dressed up and walked over to the sorority lodges in the crisp fall air. We lined up obediently and waited for the front door to open. Then we filed in, examined by the unsmiling, sharp-eyed sorority bitches inside. They broke up and filtered among us, all under the cheery guise of "getting to know you better!" But I knew what this was—military-style interrogation with an annoying pink bow on top. They were culling the herd based on any slight or imagined misstep. I chatted with some strange senior, reading her face while I talked about where I was from and what I liked to do, wondering if what I said was right and if I looked right while saying it. She nodded and smiled. Which I was pretty sure was the kiss of death.

That night at their *90210* viewing party, which was Not to Be Missed, I sat on the couch flanked by excited, sweet-smelling girls. I watched their pretty faces in the bluish light of the TV, happy finally to belong. But the thing I didn't know yet was that sorority girls do not love clever sardonic commentary inserted into their serious teen dramas. They did not want *Mystery Science Theater 3000*. When the dialogue was sweet, you went *awww*. When it was exciting, you squealed. What you couldn't do, however, was make high-pitched mewing sounds while Kelly was talking, or ask Brandon out loud if his vagina was hurting. I was met with shut-ups and threats.

"If you don't like it, just leave," someone said. I turned to see who said it, and it was my very own hall mate, the girl I came with. She did not look back. She was trying to hear what Dylan was saying to Brenda.

I withdrew into hurt silence, trying to regroup. How could I make it up to them, show them I was safe to hang with? While I tried to think of a way, I called Justin to complain about how stupid girls were.

When he picked up, I recoiled at the syrupy female laughter in the background.

"Oh, that's just . . . Joe's friends," said Justin.

"Oh, we're not your friends now, Justin?" I heard a girl say. Justin muffled the phone.

"I'm sorry, yes, I'm your friend." He laughed. "Stop that."

"Who are they?" I pouted.

"Oh, um, Katherine and Carrie."

The girl: "Cara!"

"Sorry, Cara and Katherine."

"I gotta go."

"Wait. What's wrong?"

"You're busy. Call me later."

"Wait," he demanded, tone changed. He slipped away from the noise. "What's wrong? Why did you go quiet?"

"I'm not quiet."

"Why would I be too busy to talk to you?"

"You're not. I just thought, you know. *Cara* and *Katherine*."

A long, brooding silence.

"Don't move," he said, apparently mobilizing for an intervention. "I'll be right over."

The phone clicked. My pouting had worked! He was coming over! He must really really like me. I preened myself in the mirror and dabbed on perfume as my roommate watched with dull-eyed curiosity.

But when the knock came, I found a very different Justin at the door. He strode in, seizing my head in both hands, backing me up against the wall. My roommate scuttled into her corner.

"What is wrong with you?" he growled, voice low.

"What?"

"Why are you so weak?"

"Weak?"

"Yes! WEAK." He seemed on the verge of tears. I tried to follow along.

"Well, I . . . I . . . guess I was . . . jealous?"

"No. You don't know this guy. That's. Not. Me."

I tried to calm him by nodding.

"When I love someone, I mean it. What happened to you? Why don't you trust?"

"Wait, you love me?"

Then we kissed hard, and my roommate's sunken eyes sank deeper.

Justin and I pulled out of lip-lock, breathing hard. I gestured toward the corner.

"Oh, hey," Justin said, walking over to her bedside and extending his hand. "My name's Justin."

It wasn't just me who got roughly psychoanalyzed. The problematic relationships of all people of the world were fair game. Within a half hour of meeting someone, he'd get right to why it was Mom or Dad never loved them. It pissed people off.

"Shut the fuck up about my mother," Joe would say, with a half smile on his face.

"It's because I'm right." Justin would shrug and back off. Then he'd look at me like, *why can't they see?* The truth will set them free.

When he wasn't being meaningful, or outlecturing his professors, or trying to flesh out why I was so dysfunctional, we would pass the time by making out.

Touching his chiseled body was both exciting and slightly troubling. When I lifted his shirt, it was like a Calvin Klein ad. No excess fat bulging around the waist of his jeans like I had. Just tan, hairless muscles. It was like touching a mannequin. Even his nails were flawlessly trimmed. I looked down at my own and saw gnawed, uneven nubs, chipped polish, hangnails. I slipped them behind his head and kissed harder.

Since we were both virgins, we spent a lot of time

practicing all the foreplay we'd been dying to do. Especially oral sex. As usual, Justin was overprepared. He showed up at my dorm with hard candies, toothpaste, and Bengay.

"It's ugly," I stalled, gesturing apologetically to my nether regions. "Are you sure?"

"Let me shave it," he said. "Totally bare."

"Oh, weird," I said. "The whole thing?"

"Yeah," he said. "It'd be so sexy."

"Okay, but I have to go take a shower then," I said. "I'll be right back."

"No, let me do it. We can do it here."

"You wanna shave me? Here?"

"Yeah. Please?"

His begging convinced me that it would get him off, which made sense, since it involved improving my body.

He sat my naked ass on a desk chair, pointing the warm glow of my roommate's desk light where I was sure she never intended it to shine.

He prepped like a surgeon, scrubbing up, preparing a tray with a bowl of warm water and a can of shaving foam. Face twisted with concentration, he knelt between my knees to lather up. "This won't hurt a bit," he said.

"Careful," I said, breathing through my teeth. He began to clear-cut the area, revealing contours I had not seen since childhood. It began to look less frightening, more like a Palm Beach golf course than a Connecticut swamp.

"Rest one leg up on my shoulder," he said, dipping the razor in the water. He used his thumbs to pull the skin taut, brushing the razor up and down with extreme care. I watched his face and relaxed, then started getting turned on.

Justin was too. When he was done, he calmly wiped off

the foam, inspected my sanitized form, readjusted the tent in his shorts, and dove headfirst into his masterpiece.

I reveled for a moment in the stunning heat from his mouth. Looking down, his nose atop my hairless pubic bone, I resembled a gazelle, my white flank seized in his jaws. He devoured me with psychotic intensity, sucking and licking until my knees opened, and I grabbed the now familiar Sonny Crockett burn that would shoot me out of the universe.

But I looked down at my white thighs, the rolls of my belly, the alarming signposts of my imperfect body, and froze up.

What did it taste like down there? What did it smell like? He probably hated it.

"I love it," Justin assured me, on cue. I tried to breathe.

What would Mom think? She would be SO horrified.

Stop stop *stop*. She's twelve hundred miles away.

I lay back, scrolling through my list of fantasies. Maybe if I pretended he wasn't there at all, or that I wasn't there, or that I was watching him going down on some other girl. Or that I was someone else, someone more beautiful. Or: that I was Justin—Justin doing it to a supermodel whose pussy tasted like peaches with whipped cream. Okay, that kinda worked. My body and I were erased from the screen, and it was just Peaches the Supermodel getting tied up and there's a line of guys fighting to go down on her. Safe in that thought, I lost it, exploding into a brief arc of pleasure, a shooting star that blazed up and out into darkness, before returning me to the desk chair with an abrupt thud, right where it'd found me.

• • •

While the girls back at my dorm attended parties and awaited their new Greek assignments, I was walking around campus amazed at the sensation of a completely bare twat. It was like being five years old again, only with tits and a boyfriend. And a sex drive. I went to classes in a short skirt and a thong, sat down with my legs uncrossed. I had the overpowering sensation that if I bent over to pick up my pen, everything in a two-mile radius would fuck me from behind. I slipped into a bathroom stall just to feel it, the softest, most naughty body part imaginable. I was wet for my own pussy. I rushed back to Justin's dorm to sit on his face before the stubble set in.

"That felt amazing," Justin sighed, after we'd completed the second 69 of the day. We were sprawled together in his bunk, drifting off into a deep sleep, when:

"Can I ask you something?"

My eyes flew open.

"Sure," I answered.

"Have you ever done that before?"

"What?" Uh-oh. Oh no. I knew what was about to happen. Remain calm. Breathe. Redirect.

"Like, gone down on a guy before?" he asked.

"Have you?" I asked quickly. "I mean, on a girl?"

But Justin of course had taken the high road, obsessing over many a girl but never touching, treating his crushes instead like asexual princesses, vowing to protect them while he channeled his libido into martial arts and weight lifting and squeezing the grease out of salad croutons, and beating the crap out of his penis with alternating hands, to ensure muscular symmetry in both forearms.

I propped up to look lovingly into his eyes, explaining

how important it had been for me to wait until marriage. To wait until my soul mate came along.

Dissatisfied, Justin prodded, and so I told him a little about Alex, briefly outlining that we did some stuff, but he wasn't *special* to me like this. Not like Justin.

"What kind of stuff?" Justin asked, his jaw jutting slightly, his eyes unhappy.

"Third-base stuff."

"Third-base stuff," Justin kidded nervously. "What, did you suck his dick?"

"What?" I laughed, a little too hard. "Oh, my gosh, are you kidding?"

"No." Justin pouted. "Did you?"

I said nothing, fearing he had the ability to read my mind.

Justin's lip began to tremble. "Oh, no," he managed.

"Fine, yes, once," I scolded. "But we never had sex!"

"Oh, God." Justin's voice cracked and he crumpled like he'd just been stabbed. "Once?"

"Once," I assured him. "Or twice."

"Oh, God," Justin repeated, his eyes tearing up. "So, a lot. Okay. Did he do it back to you? Did he at least give you *pleasure*?"

"Um," I said. "Justin."

"What?" he persisted, slightly crazed. "Did he make you come?"

"No, he didn't. He tried. So I kinda faked it. But look!" I brightened. "It's okay now! I finally learned to masturbate and have real orgasms so I will never fake again!"

"You sucked his DICK," Justin roared, then covered his face, quaking with abrupt little sobs. "And you . . . oh, God . . ."

Oh, shit, I thought. This was so not going as planned.

"Oh, God," he said, muffled. "Why?"

"For the rest I waited for you!" I soothed. "I never had sex with anyone!"

"It's not about the sex part!"

I thought, *Oh, yes it is.* I hadn't even gotten to the part about blowing my fellow counselor last year at church camp. I'd have to carry that one to my grave.

"It's about *dick sucking*!" he cried. "Why did you stay with him, give yourself to him, when he didn't care about you? Take care of you?"

Take care of me? I wondered. That sounded strange. Like I was some big overgrown baby. Maybe I was. Maybe it was his job to make sure I never felt any more pain, ever again. That would be, like, totally great.

"Was he bigger than me?" Justin snapped, just when I thought it couldn't get any worse. It was like a girl asking if she was fat. You just don't do it. I reeled for a minute in the power of Justin's self-worth, which was now resting limply in my hands like an injured puppy.

"No," I lied. "Of course not."

Justin looked relieved.

It was what I would've wanted to hear if I was a guy. Plus, Justin wasn't small, it was just that Alex was unnaturally endowed. Nothing could ever be that big, I was pretty sure, other than certain genetically modified cucumbers I'd noticed in the produce aisle. Not like his hugeness had ever done me any good, other than giving me the first signs of TMJ. Ugh. Maybe I was a total slut. And yet still a virgin! A virgin slut! Despite all my best efforts, I had arrived at my bridegroom with all my petals pawed and sniffed.

"I didn't make it to you in time," Justin moaned,

hanging his head, tears falling. I'd never seen a guy cry before. Maybe it was a good sign. Or a really bad one. "Why didn't I make it to you in time?"

When I couldn't give him a good answer, he took to praying on his knees, right in front of the bed, begging for supernatural guidance. Sometimes Justin communed with Buddha, sometimes with his Spirit Guide, sometimes the God of Abraham. But right now, judging by the folded hands, it looked to be Jesus.

"Why wasn't I there to save her?" he asked. "Why?"

"It wasn't that bad," I interrupted.

"Wasn't that bad?" Justin retorted hoarsely, wiping away tears. "Wasn't that BAD?" His pain redoubled. "YOU SUCKED SOME GUY'S DICK."

"Shhh," I hissed.

"AND HE DIDN'T EVEN CARE ABOUT YOU."

"I've been weak," I said, touching his short, coarse hair. "A weak, stupid person. If I'd known there was someone like you, I would've waited to do all that stuff."

We both knew that was bull. But it was supposed to be true.

"I love doing it with you," I offered. Justin backed away angrily.

"You don't have to do that to be *loved*!" he sobbed. "God!"

To highlight the point, and vent his protective anger, he stood and began practicing his tae kwon do forms in the air, probably punching an imaginary Alex. I watched, drenched in guilt, afraid to move a muscle.

Then he stopped. He paced in a circle and sighed. Then he opened his minifridge, pulled out his box of chicken tenders to squeeze, and began reading silently from his pocket-size *Tao Te Ching*. Uneasy silence returned. After a moment or two, I breathed, stretched out a bit, and cautiously reached for his *Men's Health* magazine. But Justin snatched it away and looked at me, his eyes suddenly brimming with a single, fiery message from God. I braced.

"That will never happen to you again!" he growled. "I promise!"

"I know," I said, and then, because I didn't know what else to say: "Thank you."

To pledge his fealty, and to prevent any further unwanted blow jobs, he had to fuck my brains out. I understood. I was cool with that. It was time.

While he prayed for guidance, I checked the calendar and realized the next closest holiday that could suffice as our Special Night of First Penetration was Halloween. It wasn't exactly holy, like a wedding. But Justin was so freakin' pure it didn't even matter. The wedding would come later, and it would be great. They would dance in circles to "Hava Nagila," lifting us both up in chairs, and then I'd read aloud my favorite apostle Paul quotes from the New Testament, and all his Jewish relatives would get chills. Cats and dogs would hump each other and doves would fly out of my ass. But until then, God approved of our premarital coitus because He knew our hearts and our shared destiny. He knew we were special spiritual people with special spiritual caveats to the rules.

So on Halloween night, while boisterous crowds streamed out of the dorms toward the Costume Ball, I slipped into Justin's room with the sound track to *Basic Instinct* and a brown sack of Extra Strength Trojans. Justin stood in a towel at the TV, freshly showered and ready for me. And holding up a VHS of *The Little Mermaid*.

"Hi, beautiful." He flashed me a knowing smile. "Got my favorite movie."

There were candles burning on his roommate's desk, and we were about to have sex to Walt Disney, but whatever. I had found my soul mate! My future husband! Let the fucking commence!

We stripped down nude, equal parts hard and wet, and tumbled into the bottom bunk to go through the motions of foreplay until we were nearly delirious. As Ariel swung into the final refrain of "Part of Your World," Justin timed-out to try on his first condom, carefully pinching the top and rolling it down per health class, checking and double-checking for tearproofness. Then, for luck, he ripped another one open and rolled it down over the first. I watched, speechless.

"Can't be too safe," he explained. "Ready?"

"Ready."

He laid over me and eased his crinkly, spermicide-drenched, double-bagged member into place. I put my hand down to spot the first set.

"Okay?" he asked.

"Yeah."

I looked at how hard he was and braced for the worst, chanting: relax, relax, *relax*. Then he was in, deep and warm and tight. Full, finally, instead of empty and aching.

"Oh," I said, enlightened. "Oh."

He rocked his hips just a little, intent on proving that pain and blood were for yellow-belt lovers. His breathing roared by my ear, but I could still hear all the condoms crackling loudly, like we were scrumping on a plastic tarp. Even still, the pleasure of softly giving in to his erection was unreal. When I moaned outright he pushed all the way in and began thrusting, which made the metal bunk frame tap the wall out of time with Sebastian's stupid singing.

Justin dropped his eyes and watched my tits swinging around. I was making strange, guttural cries. He shrugged and twitched, determined to keep it together.

"Okay?" he managed, like we were taking cover in an earthquake.

"Yeah!" I yelled. "Oh, yeah!"

Not only okay but too damn much. I was speared, my knees by my ears, grinding against him in a tiny little circle. I didn't even need to pretend I was someone else; my hips levitated beat by beat off the bed and into a full-body orgasm that spurred me to holler like a dismembered duck, loud enough for everyone in the Pit to enjoy.

Justin's face was red and his neck veins puffed, his eyes rolled back and he roared like Satan himself, falling face-first into my neck, where he hummed and chuckled. I reached my hand down to check the shrink-wrapping and found he was already checking it. Secure.

"Thank God," we said in unison.

After sex came more sex. Most of my memories of that freshman year were of Justin fucking me from behind, or upside down, or using the top bunk to brace himself as I screamed, "Harder . . . HARDER!" We were either doing that, emptying the free condom bucket at the campus health clinic, or using his mom's credit card to eat massive amounts of food at three in the morning. Within weeks, we were sleeping in the same bed every single night. We had to constantly be stroking arms, or holding hands, or lying on each other. We were prime candidates for a conjoined toilet. I knew this, but was powerless to stop it. I needed togetherness way more than dignity.

Joe put up with us. He was in awe of Justin's trash can, which was always overflowing with condom wrappers.

"Holy shit!" he'd holler, picking up the can to count them. He'd carry it down the hall. "Look at this." Random guys from two floors up would make the pilgrimage downstairs just to view the spoils of our Trojan War.

I barely visited my dorm at all. I returned occasionally to do laundry or swap out my textbooks. When I did, I made it quick, hurrying past rooms of girls I'd barely gotten to know before I'd become an unknown again, *the girl who is never here.* Box fans were spinning in their windows, music and laughter in the air, sorority pledge thingies hanging on the walls. Someone popped their head out and said "hi" to me as I passed. I waved back weakly, embarrassed.

I opened my door and greeted my sullen, reclusive roommate and summed up my side of the room. There were cobwebs on the windowsill; a few notes by my phone saying my parents had called the week before. I rummaged through the toiletries on my dust-covered counter and gathered some clean underwear from my drawer. Then I picked up my phone and dialed into my voicemail.

"Hey it's me," came Mom's recorded voice. "Listen I left you the number to the Atlanta Church of Christ, did you get it? They have an eleven o'clock service on Sunday. It looks like a really great program, and it's not far from you at all. I think you should go."

Sighing, I punched the keypad and moved on to the next.

"It's me again." Her voice was irritated. "I'm not sure why I can't get ahold of you. It's seven thirty. I've called three times."

I shuddered and clicked the receiver, not wanting to hear the next seven messages. I already knew. I dialed her number and sat on the edge of my unfamiliar bed, my body as stiff as the mattress. My roommate flipped pages under the glow of her defiled desk lamp, not listening to my every move. I turned away to look out the window. This place didn't smell like me at all. My clothes and my blankets had absorbed the concrete walls and stale carpeting.

I twisted the cord in my fingers, waiting through the rings.

When Mom answered, I jumped to life, trying hard to sound like myself, gushing about my new boyfriend, my classes, my clothes, anything I could think of to put her at ease. I needed to be absolved, to reassure her that things were normal, that I was utilizing my new shower tote and shoe rack as appropriate, just like if this was camp.

"Church of Christ?" I said, a little too eagerly. "Eleven o'clock? Super! I'll have to check it out!"

I left out a few details, like the part about how I was known as "the screamer" at Justin's dorm, and how sometimes his friends graded our performance by sliding a 7.5 under our locked door.

Mom didn't need to know the truth. After all, I wasn't in danger. I was still close to Jesus. I still prayed. Hell, wasn't Justin proof that God had answered me? It's just, without the airlock of parental supervision, things had gotten a bit scattered. A few important balloons had gone fishtailing into space. Like my virginity. And my grip on reality. And my ability to use regular verbs and adjectives. Other than that, everything was great.

"Fuckin' A," I said to myself one day. "Holy shit. Holy fuckin' shit!"

"Uh-oh." Justin laughed. "Now you're going to hell."

But hell was child's play compared to the freak flag of verbal nonrestraint I was about to unfurl. It seemed I couldn't put even the smallest sentence together in standard English anymore.

"Can you fucking believe that?" I'd say, pointing at something, anything.

It wasn't the salt I wanted you to pass me, it was the motherfucking salt. It wasn't an essay I had to write, it was a bitchfest of cocknobbery. It wasn't crazy, it was shitballs, it was twat-cockin', piss-fucking snatch-munching fucknuts!

Maybe it was Justin's Palm Beachesque affinity for gangsta rap. Since I spent a lot of time lying around and watching Justin shadowbox in his room, I received a daily education on Pharcyde and Tupac.

He'd stop, out of breath, to look at me.

"Did you hear that lyric?" he asked, breathing hard. "Wait, listen again. The sample and the hook right there on 'motherfuckin' cap that nigga'—it's brilliant." He'd pause it and play back the phrase twice, three times. Soon, the lankiest, whitest of all white girls was riding around representin' in the Bronco: "I ain't got time for bitches," I rapped into the rearview. "Gotta keep my mind on my mothafuckin' riches."

When I wasn't being White Girlz in da Hood, I was studying modern misogyny with Justin for our advanced women's studies class we were taking together. We took all the same classes. We sat side by side in the computer lab, so we could hug every five minutes and then play Doom until midnight. When we were done, we'd go to the cafeteria and he'd watch me eat frozen yogurt and try to figure out what was wrong with me.

"Why do you hate yourself?" he asked me.

"What, it's fucking low-fat!"

"No, not the yogurt," he said, and then with meaning: "I'm still *haunted*."

Oh. The blow jobs again. I stuck my spoon in my cup and sighed. My poor, poor disappointed future husband.

He would shake his head with the sad, burdened heart of the philosopher-king. He teared up again, blamed my low self-esteem on the Church of Christ, my parents, my ex-boyfriends. But despite these comforting explanations, and me constantly stuffing his cock in my mouth as consolation, the only thing that seemed to make up for him not having been there for me in the past was never ever separating in the present. We sat on the curb in front of his dorm, trying to part for the night, yawning, hugging.

"Bye," we'd say, and not move.

Sometimes we'd lie in the grass beside the fire hydrant, spooning, drifting in and out of sleep. We'd wake up at four a.m. as the partiers were stepping over us on their way into the dorm. Still couldn't let go. It was nauseating to everyone but us.

"They're jealous," Justin pointed out, picking grass out of my hair. I knew what he meant. Our true love transcended the world's superficial rules. "Just come sleep at my place. Why are we fighting it? It's stupid."

"But what if my motherfucking parents call, nigga?"

"I'll set the alarm and you can come back here real early."

I loved how he didn't want to let me go. Loved it. Why should we have to be alone if we didn't want to, homie? It was college; we could make our own rules. But at his dorm, after five hours of three new positions, with his roommate cursing his life in the top bunk, I always slept past the alarm. Morning calls from my mother went unanswered and suspicion brewed at home.

The ultimate reckoning was a weekend visit from Mom and Grandma.

It wasn't like I didn't know they were in town. I just couldn't bring myself to sleep apart from Justin, not even for one night.

"It's our right to be together," Justin comforted me, as we made love and drifted off to sleep.

Early that Sunday morning, Mom and Grandma drove over from their hotel room to my dorm, ready to pick me up for the long awaited eleven o'clock service at the local Church of Christ. But instead of me, she found my empty bed exactly as she'd left it in September, only covered with a cryptlike layer of dust.

My roommate, the human mole, peeked out from behind her covers.

"She's never here," she said.

While I slept peacefully on Justin's hairless chest, a contented smile playing on my lips, my seething mother was on the other side of the campus, pacing the halls of my dorm asking where on earth her daughter was. Someone told her, slipped her the phone number where I could be found cohabiting. Cue the worst possible introduction to my future husband.

"Justin, I don't know who you think you are," came the voice mail in his room, "and I don't care to ever meet you, but I have never been so disgraced in all my life. Please tell my daughter to get her *butt* in gear and get ready for CHURCH."

"Crap," Justin said, which pretty well summed up the situation.

Blurry with adrenaline, I raced over to my dorm in yesterday's clothes, panicked for an excuse. Justin's name, now in red at the top of the shit list, and he hadn't even had time to bow cutely for her, the way he did when he met people for the first time. I wouldn't even get to explain how he was a black belt. And a Jew who loved Jesus.

As I approached my mom, all remnants of tough gangsta sex queen evaporated, leaving only a pale little suburban girl with really bad bed head.

"Do you think I'm stupid?" Mom growled at me. Grandma waited outside my dorm door, picking lint off of her cardigan while my roommate's hollow eyes followed along in silence. My mom hurled a dress at me, wondering aloud why it was costing her so much to pay for a dorm that I did not use because I was too busy being a complete slut.

"I swear," I said, hanging my head, not sure what I was swearing about. "I swear."

"This was a *mistake*!" she hissed, with such visceral anger I wasn't sure if she meant her visit, the university, or my birth.

There's a place for us, the angels sang softly, just like Barbra Streisand. *Somewhere, a place for us.*

I couldn't wait to run to Justin to bemoan my mistreatment, my subjection to the more barbaric forms of Christianity, to the unfairness of my family.

Not long after that, my parents and I stopped speaking. I'd done such a good job being palatable for eighteen years that they were quite ill-prepared for the tsunami of my New Love. The day Mom discovered my stash of birth control pills and condoms was a dark day in our family history. I was pretty sure it would've been better if she'd caught me smoking crack with hookers. At least with that, one can rehabilitate a person. But how do you cure an addiction to Jewish cock in extra-ribbed tropical fruit flavors?

"What do you think people think of you?" came Mom's tearful, leading question, with only one answer. They thought I was weird. Hell, I thought I was weird. But I'd been weird my whole life and was only getting weirder. My battle plan was deny, deny, deny.

"I bought the condoms just in case," I said.

"Just in case what? The world supply runs out?"

In reality, I just wanted them to stop talking to me about sex, to stop picturing me having sex, so I could stop picturing them picturing me having sex while we actually had sex, which I couldn't help but do since it had become such a monumentally big, bad deal.

Then it started: the mystery sex pain. It was just a little tinge on the downward thrust, a bad burn that threatened to get worse if we didn't time-out.

"What is it?" Justin asked, looking down at me.

"Maybe I'm getting an infection," I said. "I'll get it checked out."

But when it turned out I had nothing wrong with me, other than an apparent deficiency of K-Y Jelly, I was left to ponder what mystery ailment, besides the looming apparition of Mom and Dad's unhappy faces, had crept its way into my sex.

"My mom's a therapist," Justin explained. "Talk to her. She's very open about sex. And she doesn't care if I marry someone who's not Jewish."

"Doubt that."

"You'll see. On spring break, we're driving to my house."

• • •

Sure enough, Justin's mom—the open-minded therapist—waited for our arrival with open-minded arms.

"I made you a bed up in the room down the hall." She winked as we dragged our suitcase of condoms inside. "That way you can tell your mom you're sleeping down there."

In the morning, she brought orange juice on a tray to our bed. That was great, but also kinda not-so-great. It was one thing to be doing it doggy-style on your future mother-in-law's guest bed, and quite another to have her replenishing your electrolytes between positions.

She also presented me with the latest edition of *Our Bodies, Ourselves*. It had the biggest and boldest diagrams of sexual positions I had ever seen. There was a whole chapter on contraception. Another one with dark pictures of botched abortions. And pages upon pages on female masturbation.

"There's also a section in there on codependency," she said. "I think you should read it."

Justin came in just then to nuzzle in my neck.

"Me wan coh dohs," he baby-talked. "Coh dohs."

"You wanna *cuddle* with me?" I goo-gooed back.

"Coh dohs," he repeated.

"Like I was saying," his mom continued, swallowing a little vomit, "I think two people can be too close."

"Coh doh!" Justin whimpered.

"It's coh doh time." I giggled, and we ran off to 69 in her shower. "Thanks for the book!"

It had arrived a little too late.

14 | The Great Band-Aid in the Sky

"The Holy Spirit came on them, and they began speaking in tongues and prophesying."

—ACTS 19:6

Justin and I were together for four years, and every year that passed, our spirituality grew and blossomed like a flower. Or a limb with elephantiasis. Or a mushroom cloud that amazes you, right before it incinerates your eyeballs and turns your head into fertilizer.

We had become devout Christians. Not just any kind of devout, either. We were into the mystical stuff. The crazy shit. The trapdoor that led directly to Jehovah. In order to get there, we had to do special things, like get baptized a lot. Like get real comfortable speaking in tongues. And most important: We had to get the anointing. We had to get healed. And by "we," we meant me.

At the time, getting healed seemed to us like the best way to help my chronically poor self-image, while getting Justin the training he needed to rule the world. He had studied televangelists closely and decided there was definitely something to it, some energy field these guys were tapping into, some trick of nature or physics that anyone could master with enough dedication.

A few times, Justin practiced on me.

"It's about belief," he explained, practicing his deep breathing. "You erase all doubt and extend chi through the wall."

Then he placed his hands on my back and made several sharp blowing sounds.

"They feel warm!" I told him, concentrating. "I think I feel it! I think I felt your chi!"

"Hmm." Justin nodded. "Yeah, but. Still not enough. We need *him*."

He nodded at the TV, at the luminous ivory Armani suit of Benny Hinn, the best of the best on the Anointed Jesus Supersquad circuit. Benny Hinn could heal the hell out of people, send them bouncing out of their wheelchairs and straight onto the ropes of Cirque du Soleil. Justin was sure that if we flew to Hinn headquarters in Saviourland, wherever that was, and he presented himself as a disciple, bowing cutely with a very serious expression, the televangelist would intuitively sense his latent spiritual power and invite him into his Superpowers Healing Preschool. The problem was that Hinn had so much anointing he required bodyguards and security clearances. We needed easier access.

So we started out at the mostly black megacathedral in South Atlanta. The World Anointers rose like a bronze coliseum amid gutted strip malls and run-down fast-food joints. We followed the streaming throngs and shuttle buses, and walked inside to find several tiers of unsmiling greeters who reminded us in a gently threatening way to remove thy gum. They handed out tissues, for tears of joy or infection control, I wasn't sure which. We were quickly ushered into the purple-carpeted stadium, which vibrated with the most sublime gospel singing I'd ever heard.

"Run to God," they sang in gorgeous ten-part harmony. "Run to God."

Must run, I thought involuntarily, lifting my hands in the air. That was how you received a direct transmission to the most high without a Walkman, by holding your hands high and blubbering in tongues. I closed my eyes and joined in.

"Homina-homina-homina-homina," I hummed, trying not to appear scared shitless. "Labia-labia-labia-labia-labai-labai-adonai!"

Pastor Creflo Dollar took the podium, followed by the long arm of an aerial TV camera, and the massive space thundered to life.

If preachers had superpowers, then Creflo's would've been the gift of decryption. Like a Magic 8 Ball, he could look at any Bible verse on any given page and decode the hidden message about your finances, your depression, even your herpes.

"Jeremiah, Chapter One, verse five," said Pastor, speaking with calm, good-humored authority. " 'Before I formed thee, I knew thee, I sanctified thee, I ordained thee'—people: He knew you and He chose you! Before the foundations of the earth! You were born for a time such as this! You were alive for a time such as this! God knew . . . He *knew* that He had to have the best running in the fourth leg of the relay race! You are here right now for a reason!"

The crowd roared around me, lifting the hairs on the

back of my neck. I was sold. In the gift shop, I would put down all my cash to buy the Creflo box set of sermons on *Healing the Demon of Low Cash Flow.*

But Justin wasn't satisfied. "He's good." He shrugged. "But not the man we need."

As it turned out, through a creepy Jesus-loving hobo friend (of which Justin had several) he'd found our man, Pastor Tim Storey. Tim had once worked for Benny Hinn catching healed people as they fell onstage. He was a *catcher,* and as such had caught the anointing, much like an exciting spiritual STD, and was currently on a speaking tour preaching at a Pentecostal hole-in-the-wall four hours away in Asheville. Without hesitation we packed Justin's gun collection, his matching fanny pack holsters, all my makeup and curling irons, and headed north.

At the Holy Tabernacle of Wonderment, which was a corrugated tin trailer, we sat riveted in the front row, Justin the soon-to-be-anointed Jew, and me, his soon-to-be-serotonin-balanced white girl. The margins of our newly purchased Bibles were already chock-full of scribbles and our verses were well highlighted. As Tim Storey came up on the stage, we popped the caps off of our pens and sat with bated breath.

"He looks just like you!" I whispered to Justin, clutching his nonwriting hand.

Justin looked back and nodded, smiling big. It was not uncommon for us to see Justin in everything that was impressive—brilliant professors, successful doctors, famous dead people, a slice of cheesecake.

At the end of Pastor Storey's sermon, I ran up onstage to receive my portion, to be cleansed of my ugliness and cured of my fear of sleeping alone, my codependence, my flatulence, the list went on and on. I'm not sure what Justin wanted to be healed of. I don't think he really needed to be fixed so much as activated. Like Frankenstein.

As I mounted the steps, Pastor stretched out his arm, eyes rolling up into his head like Moses before the Red Sea.

"Signs and Wonders through your hands!" he cried out to me, and long distance zapped me with what I imagined to be a can of God's very own whup-ass. I didn't really feel the whup, but I felt something a notch above grocery shopping. Which was a problem. I didn't get knocked down. I was *supposed* to get knocked down. Holy shit, what the fuck was I supposed to do now? I hadn't done enough anointment pre-planning. There was a protocol when being healed, and moseying off the stage with your hands in your pockets was so not it. Thinking quick, I listed to the right and improvised a standing triple lutz, disintegrating near the podium, where I landed on my back.

I blinked up at the stage lights. I figured it was okay if I faked it a little. I'd still been touched by God. I tingled with wonderment just thinking about how my DNA was probably rewiring and renewing, soaking up the energetic baptism. *Thud. Thud.* More bodies crumbled to the floor around me.

But when should I, like, *get up*?

Should I play dead?

Should I get up now?

How about now?

The other healees were still twitching like just-caught fish. How long did it take for the average wave of God to pass through? If I got up too early, would I be asked to lie back down? Should I appear woozy? Exhilarated?

Unsure, I lay frozen, hoping for clues, afraid to lift my

head and look around, or move my hands to a more comfortable position, or inch my body to safety.

I hoped Pastor Storey would not step on me, or be embarrassed, seeing as how he was still preaching, and I was splayed out by his feet with my dress near my ears. But who was I to question what God hath set in place.

Signs and wonders, bitches. *Signs and motherfucking wonders.*

15 | Won't the Real Savior Please Stand Up

> "And the person who keeps every law of God,
> but makes one little slip, is just as guilty as a
> person who has broken every law there is."
>
> —JAMES 2:10

My life with fresh anointment was very sparkly. It lasted for about three hours.

It fell off when I returned to our one-bedroom off-campus apartment where we lived with Joe and Joe's moldy plates, which he kept in the closet by the keg.

I had lied to my parents and told them I wasn't shacking up with Justin anymore. I didn't want to dupe them so much as I just wanted to see the color return to their faces, to see them experiencing the abiding peace that cometh with having a well-adjusted daughter, whose boyfriend wasn't the center of her entire existence.

Earlier that year, as reward for lying convincingly, they'd paid for a nice little off-campus dorm room for me, which even came with some nice, pre-assigned female roommate, what's-her-name, and I, in my newly acquired old-soul wisdom, would live there with her about as long as it took Mom and Dad to drive back to the airport.

When the coast was clear, I frantically mined my closet for clothes and fled back to Justin's apartment, leaving behind only tinkling wire hangers, like the skeleton of my identity. At Justin's, my skirts and T-shirts and platform shoes were stuffed into the coat closet next to all his shiny basketball jerseys.

I hated the possibility that I'd been reduced to nothing more than his groupie. Just because I cried every time he left my side to go to his kung fu class, or to the store, or the bathroom, that didn't make me a groupie. I couldn't help that when we were apart, I felt like I was dead. I'd crumple on his kitchen floor sobbing, daydreaming about cutting my wrists so he'd come home and find me bloody and dead, and be sorry that he'd ever left.

But what would actually happen is, I'd finally get up off the dirty vinyl, fix my mascara, and drive over to my empty apartment, where I'd make my weekly call to Mom so she'd continue to believe that I was happier than ever, and not living in both sin and misery simultaneously.

"Did you get the Dr. Laura book I sent you?" she asked.

You mean the devil's manifesto?

"Yeah," I said, disliking how my voice echoed off the bare walls and empty cabinets. A few of my old skirts had been left out on my bed for so long that the sun had actually bleached out the pattern in the shape of the window. "I got the book right here."

Ten Stupid Things Women Do to Mess Up Their Lives, screamed the title. I cringed at the bloodred cover. Somebody was trying to convince me that premarital cohabitation was unpaid prostitution. Somebody was trying to wean me off my life support. But oh no. Not going out like that.

I'd cracked the book a tad, not all the way, and skimmed the sections Mom had highlighted, some case study about a stupid, needy woman who'd married a drug addict and had kids with him. *Ha ha ha,* I gloated as I read. *What a dumbass.* Note to self: *DOES NOT APPLY.*

Then I turned the page and was, in mid-sentence, skull-fucked by the exact diagnosis of my own malfunction: *Dependent. Defined by men. Cop-out. No independent goals.* I read quickly, for fear if I paused too long my eyes would snag on one of Mom's fluorescent yellow exclamation points and bleed from sheer guilt. The basic gist was, I embodied nine out of ten stupid things women do to mess up their lives. I was the poster child for Stupid Women. Maybe Dr. Laura had a point. But dammit, so did I. I just wasn't sure what mine was yet. And I wasn't going to figure it out with a book that made my eyes bleed.

"You ought to read it," Mom was still saying. "She's so good. She really tells it like it is."

"Or like *she* sees it."

"She's Jewish, you know."

"What, do you still think I'm living with Justin? I told you I wasn't."

Daring to talk back to my mother was new territory. It made me sweat and shake all over.

"But I can never get hold of you. What on earth are you doing?"

Shacking up and having sex! I screamed silently. *Dedicating my life to God!*

"Just stuff!" I bellowed. Because how could I possibly do both and still do either.

But on Friday nights, while normal college kids did bong hits and played Mortal Kombat, we were doing laundry and studying our Bibles for our World Anointers Bible class. Because in order to become megachurch megamembers, we had to become mega-Christians, which meant committing to all the tenets of Christianity and accepting them without question, forever and ever amen.

Justin wasted no time assimilating all the rules and regs, arranging all the important Bible stories into his own self-created philosophical paradigm, which he would then deconstruct for me in little folksy wisdoms. Like, with Sodom and Gomorrah.

"I mean, as a man, you have to understand," Justin tried to explain, dragging his highlighter across Genesis 19. "Something about a guy fucking a guy." He paused for emphasis. "It's just *wrong.* Y'know?"

Maybe I was just dense. I couldn't figure out how the same God who so loved the world that He gave His only begotten son to it could also hate some of it so much He'd nicknamed it the "abomination." Abomination was like fifty points worse than "sinner." An abomination basically meant that you were the Lord's nonlovable delinquent shit-stained bastard child, and as such He needed to wear a hazmat suit to remotely detonate your mortal soul. A soul that, incidentally, He'd created. And supposedly loved. I was so confused.

"If the Bible said it," Justin tried again, reading my blank expression, "there has to be truth in it."

What he meant was, if you can't understand it, you still have to accept it. After all, he was a Jew and he'd accepted Jesus. He was a Christian but he'd accepted reincarnation. Justin had swallowed all kinds of contraindicated doctrine, because without doing so how could he increase his chances of getting the supernatural endorsement he needed to heal the sick and defeat Skeletor? If the One Living God also wanted to be the One True Homophobe, so be it. Make it work.

But I sat there and stewed, staring down the barrel of Genesis, where the sex-crazed gays of Sodom were so horny they were begging to bang Lot's male friends, who were actually God's angels in disguise. So Lot does what any upstanding man of the Lord would do: he hands over his two young virgin daughters to the horde, and tells them, *Do whatever you want to my girls, just please: no gay sex with my friends!* A few verses later, the entire city and all of its gays were consumed by the fiery wrath of God, and all the heteros lived happily ever after. Case closed.

"Hold up, wait a minute." I tried to form the question.

The ridiculously arbitrary and moody nature of God's "wrath" notwithstanding, why would He pour it upon men for anal sex and not also upon fathers who used their daughters as human shields? What sort of loving and omniscient God kills time by tricking His people? Right before He firebombs them?

But before I could even open my mouth, I realized I already knew the answer. God didn't write that. It was probably just some guy.

Siccing torches and pitchforks on outsiders, spewing contrived propaganda, killing an entire city to purify some Country Club in the Sky? Canonizing his fear of cooties and entitling them the *Holy Word of God*? That kind of primitive douchebaggery had "straight man" written all over it.

His faith undeterred, Justin pushed his papers aside, set his pens and highlighters down on the dryer and began practicing his kung fu forms. I stared at the hard, glossy cover of his closed Bible. How could I put my whole heart behind God's wonderful promises, sandwiched as they were between page after page of contradictory logic, murderous threats and self-masturbatory filler? These were somebody's marching orders all right. Somebody's creepy journal entries. But they weren't the Almighty's. How on earth could I possibly make them mine?

On Monday I drove to the university alone. Justin and I usually took all the same classes, but more and more, I was ending up having to take my own. And as with anything that belonged solely to me, I cared less and less about it. Especially prerequisites like Astronomy 301, a class I was actively failing. But I drove to campus anyway to sit in my car at the parking deck.

I'll go in in a sec, I told myself, squinting at the lecture hall across the street. I was so late already. It would cause a huge stir, just trying to find a seat. I considered my binder on the passenger seat. The exam was coming, I'd skipped almost half the classes and had no one to beg notes from. Not wanting to ponder my nonexistent backup plan, I drifted into the Dr. Laura show on AM 750. I'd started listening to it lately. Somewhere, Mom probably was too. It made us closer somehow. And a little farther apart.

I turned up the volume just in time to hear Dr. Laura punishing a caller who'd identified herself as shacking up with her boyfriend.

"Frankly," Dr. Laura told her, "you're being lazy and self-centered."

Bristling, I leaned forward, willing the caller to fight back on my behalf.

Why does she have to get your approval, Dr. Laura? I demanded. *Why can't she just do what makes her happy?* But the caller ignored my diatribe, promising to do better, clearly bereft of any independent spirit. Just like Dr. Laura had prophesied I would become.

Cold adrenaline vibrated in my fingertips. Did I have the balls to call in? *Why,* I would ask, *did SEX put God's panties in such a fucking bunch?* Wasn't God a tad smarter, or busier, or more distracted by important things, like the business of embodying unconditional love?

A minute passed on the digital clock, and the next caller tapped in.

"I was recently raped," a woman sobbed. "And I got pregnant."

Blinding daylight glared off my dashboard but I stared into it anyway, not noticing the pain. "I've struggled so much with this, Dr. Laura. I didn't want to keep the baby. But I prayed about it with my husband, and even though it's so hard . . . we're going to keep it."

There would be no going to class today. How could I even stand up with this knife in my gut? Who cared if I passed astronomy anyway. Who cared about the science of the solar system and the infinite universe and the divine fucking plan, if the God who held it all in place was like this, forbidding a woman any of it unless she obeyed and became a captive breeding sow, her destiny bound to whatever untied beast happened to mount her that day. According to the Bible, all she had to do was trade in her sex and her freedom, and in return be yoked with the glories of indentured motherhood. All she had to do was leave her life of unpaid prostitution, and become *God's* unpaid prostitute.

"I am so proud of you," Dr. Laura gushed as the caller continued to cry. "You are my hero."

These, the principles I was to espouse if I was going to go all the way with God.

It's almost laughable, I thought, wiping tears from my eyes.

Almost. But not quite.

16 | America's Next Top Girlfriend

> ". . . be self-controlled, chaste, homemakers, good-natured, adapting and subordinating themselves to their husbands."
>
> —TITUS 2:5

I decided that I was going to give Justin the best birthday party ever. I figured it was either that or throw myself off a cliff. I'd recently gotten fired from my job slicing cow tongue at Bagelicious, so I figured now was as good a time as any to redouble my efforts into the only purpose I had left: becoming the kind of woman every man wants to fuck and/or marry.

A contender for America's Top Girlfriend—in addition to having a working vagina—spends at least 40 percent of her time cleaning her boyfriend's apartment and the remaining 60 percent avoiding looking fat or heinous; hiring strippers for house calls is also on her to-do list. These activities distract her from her complete and utter lack of purpose, while also serving to blind other males to the fact that she doesn't pay any rent.

Which is why, on Justin's twenty-first, I found myself

arranging chairs in a circle in our living room and collecting entry fees from our neighbors, the Georgia Tech guys.

"I want a girlfriend like you!" one of them said, slapping me on the ass as I counted bills.

I looked around, hoping everyone had heard that.

But when my hired stripper arrived, she was disappointingly hot.

"Where's the birthday boy?" she asked.

"Right over there," I said, slipping her a wad of twenties.

I took my rightful place in the background, where it was my job to control the boombox so she had the right beat with which to bounce and ripple her naked ass in Justin's face. I monitored his crotch for signs of arousal and pretended to laugh, suddenly nauseous.

This is what it takes to win, I scolded myself.

"Happy birthday, baby!" I shouted. "Woo hoo!"

Afterward, while our engineer friends emptied their wallets, wondering if they could pawn their textbooks to cover after-show blow-job packages, Justin pulled me into our room—an office with newspaper taped over the French doors—to pummel me with pent-up libido, which he promised was totally not for the stripper but instead all for me.

Later, when we emerged, the Tech guys were still there, hanging with Joe on the wraparound couch. Since they couldn't afford to pay for sex, they'd downgraded to watching the Braves game. And during the commercials, a DVD of back-to-back gangbang cum shots. It was basically one snot-covered female after another, each with her eyes closed, tongue thrust skyward, drowning in the abysmal rain of three to eight dudes. Then she'd smile for the camera, strings of cum dripping off her eyelashes. Around me, the guys hummed with approval.

"Why the fuck is she smiling?" I demanded, gagging. "She's covered in biohazard!"

"Shut up, you're missing the point," said Joe, forwarding to a different one. "Okay, here we go. This . . . this is the chick I was talking about."

"Can you fix my leak?" she says, and begins masturbating. This looks dangerous, considering the three-inch blades of her square-tipped acrylic nails.

"I think I can help," says her pale, sickly, pockmarked male co-star.

Within thirty seconds, she's getting rammed up the ass.

"This bitch is unbelievable," Panjhi said. Panjhi: the twangiest, most beer-swillin', confederate flag wavin' good ol' boy to ever call Sri Lanka his native home.

"Can you believe her?" he hooted. "I mean, hot damn. She's perfect."

I leaned closer. Her bottom, which was all you could see, was a tanned bread loaf of muscle and seamless puff, like she'd been dropped out of a butt-manufacturing assembly line. She thrust it aerobically toward the sorry looking dude, whose chest and waist were as saggy as hers were taut. Her boobs were like cement grapefruits, the nipples threatening to burst; one aimed toward the ceiling, the other for the wall.

"Those are fake!" I cried, my jealousy exploding.

"Those are good!" said Panjhi, with a smile that seemed hostile. She was leveraged into acrobatic positions and corked in every possible hole with all her friends and neighbors. It looked painful, but she loved it all, her pert little face hawing with ecstasy.

"If I could have that woman, I would dedicate my life to Jesus."

"You already did that last week," I muttered, wondering

what had happened to my upbeat and endearing personality.

"Hey, Justin, can you just make her shut UP for five minutes? I'm trying to have guy time," Panjhi complained.

Justin was transfixed, drinking a Sprite beside me, popping his knuckles. Without unpeeling his eyes from the screen he leaned over to me, knowing. "Don't worry. They all resent their mothers. It's obvious."

My eyes dropped to my folded legs, compressed within their denim tubes, the unsexiest things in the room. I wanted to cry. I was *never* going to look that good while getting gangbanged. I was *never* going to sprout plastic tits. It was futile. I was no longer in the running toward becoming America's Next Top Girlfriend.

I stood up and huffed out.

"What's the matter?" Justin said, finding me alone in the dark in our office of love. We were about to have the same conversation we'd had a hundred times. But if Justin lived for anything, it was to save me. He closed the door and sat down next to me on the bed.

"How can you love me," I said, wiping my eyes, "when I'll never look like that?"

"You're beautiful. I love your body."

"No, you don't," I cried. "No, I'm not."

"Yes, you are."

"No, I'm not. I know, all right?"

"Know what?"

"That you'd rather marry a girl with a better body. Any guy would."

"First of all," said Justin, putting on his best psychologist voice, "I'm not some asshole, okay? I'm Justin. Second, you have no grounding in reality. Third, you are an idiot. I cannot believe I am in love with such an idiot."

While he was good at listening and consoling his patient, Justin also contradicted himself in ways that were so subtle they were easy to ignore. For instance, his obsession with the legs of certain supermodels. Not the whole body, just the legs, just Kathy Ireland folded in half, no torso or head needed. Her tan, disembodied, manlike quadriceps were so buff that they made him convulse with longing, sometimes running to the bathroom so he could rip a hole in the magazine with his dick.

"You could bounce a quarter off her calves!" he told me, by way of explanation.

"Ah," I said, knowing that he still loved me unconditionally. But just in case he didn't, I began a new weight-lifting regimen that was sure to put me back in the running. It involved cutting my eating in half—which meant one meal every other day—and following Justin to the gym every day to kill my quads, and any other muscle that insisted on being female and flabby. Which was basically every muscle I owned.

Quadulating my toothpick legs till they nearly buckled—that I could do. But the not-eating part was hard. I lacked the self-mutilating talents of an anorexic. And though the guilt over an Oreo or two had driven me to stare down the toilet bowl, jamming my finger down my throat till my eyes watered, I was born without the ability to make puke on demand. For that I'd need a beer and two shots of tequila, then I could projectile vomit like the girl in *The Exorcist*.

So to trick myself out of caloric intake I'd have to create something far weirder, my own brand of eating disorder, like spitting my half-chewed junk food into the garbage disposal, or a Dixie cup, if one was handy. I mean, I just wanted to taste the chocolate bar, or the baklava, or the macaroni salad. Just wanted to chew it a bit, not digest it or process it as fat.

I'd wait till Justin left, and take my package of Little Debbies into the bathroom, and chew and spit, chew and spit, chew and spit. It would stand to reason that the slimy mess I created should have prompted a gag reflex, but no, not that lucky. I dumped out my cup into the toilet, flushed, took one more look at Kathy Ireland's bufftastic legs poking out of the magazine holder, and emerged from the bathroom appearing completely normal.

"Who ate all the cookies?" Justin wondered aloud.

I shrugged as though I couldn't imagine who would do something so piglike. It certainly wasn't me, systematically unloading them from their plastic cylinders and into my mouth like a human Nerf gun, so I could chew and spit them all into the trash. Boy that would be weird.

But the last—and final—test of my worthiness was Lesley.

Lesley was a high school senior from Texas who was visiting our college on a school trip. When Justin had met her, he'd looked deep into her eyes and known—beyond the shadow of a doubt—that she'd been his horse around the turn of the century, during his incarnation as a Lakota Indian. Her name had been Nee Maha. This flashback had come to him while studying a painting of pinto horses. Then he saw a horse sticker on her retainer case, and knew.

"I got her number," he told me, knowing that if anyone should be happy for him, it'd be America's Next Top Girlfriend Runner-up.

"Really?" I asked over the blaring Native American flute music. There were candles burning everywhere, enough to set off the internal sprinkler system. He'd been praying again. Holding a holy vigil. For her. I felt like I'd been kicked by a buffalo.

"I have to call her," he explained.

"Oh," I said, sullen. Justin stared at me, waiting.

"But I have to do it *alone*."

"Why can't I listen?"

"I'm sorry," Justin answered, giving me a hug, assuring me that it wasn't romantic, it was just very *karmic*. "Now could you just . . . ? Out here?"

I gathered my things and drooped against the wall outside the front door, trying not to lapse into another round of suicidal thoughts.

Justin's not bound to the rules of this world, I reminded myself. *He's deep. Very fucking deep.*

Nope, still off. Something was off. Something big. But what?

With the laser precision of a McDonald's happy meal toy, I scanned my radar over the sum total of our relationship, hunting for clues.

An hour later, when he emerged from his spiritual phone call, I still hadn't quite figured it out.

"Lesley was just so cold," he murmured, ready to cry in my lap. "She refuses to remember. Why, why, *why* am I cursed to relive this?"

"Karma?" I offered, with my cheeriest dead eyes. I felt like motor oil was dripping down my face.

"Has to be karma," he said. "Or destiny. Which is why I've decided. I have to go to Texas to see her. In person. I have to. Her spring break is coming up and . . ."

His voice was drowned out by the sound of a bus, running over my head.

"What'd you just say?" I asked.

"Listen, I wish to God I didn't have to go see her," he soothed. "But I do."

Suddenly I saw it. Justin and I had no future. The healings, the public prayers in the food court, the Bible studies, the kung fu, the past lives—I didn't want it anymore. I didn't want to be a close second. I didn't want to exist only as a prop in someone else's adventure.

"If you leave," I managed, "things will never be the same when you come back."

"There is nothing sexual going on!" He laughed, incredulous. "It's like . . . it's like . . . *going to see my little sister!*"

I started to cry, wiping my eyes on my sleeve.

"C'mere," said Justin. "So dramatic."

"I'm serious," I warned, pressing my fist against his shoulder as he pulled me in. I hated how he talked like that, even if he was right.

"If I don't do this," he went on, "I'll always wonder. Before I can be totally yours, I need to see what this feeling is about."

This *feeling*?

"I gotta get out of here," I sniffed, not knowing where I was going. Maybe he'd beg me to stay.

"Bye, beautiful," he said, the way you call to a pouting child. "Don't I get a hug?"

"No" I called back and closed the front door behind me.

I could feel him shrugging it off. He was used to me running away. He'd talk me out of it later. And if he couldn't, well. There was always Lesley.

I walked to my car, oppressed by the dusty blue evening sky overhead. It reminded me of Texas. I pictured a natural blond, calm and petite, riding horses around her ranch, a brief composite sketch of everything I wasn't. *How fucking boring is that*, I thought, and sagged. They'd probably hold hands while eating Texas-style BBQ, and Justin would stare into Lesley's eyes with honey-glazed sincerity, the same way he'd stared into mine.

I unlocked my Cavalier, pushed the crumpled wrappers onto the floor and collapsed into the driver's seat. I waited for the sadness and grief to hit me, but nothing came. I pulled the door shut hard and waited.

Still nothing.

You don't want him anymore, that's why. I waited for this blasphemy to trigger an earthquake of sobs, but nothing stirred. There was only a little glimmer of relief, a flash of me in my natural state, undiluted by Justin. I seemed happier.

I put the key in the ignition, and nodded to whoever would become my inevitable replacement, conceding defeat. The windows of Justin's apartment stared back, unconcerned.

I need to see what this feeling is about, he'd said.

"I think I do too," I sighed, and the engine revved to life.

17 | Special Forces

> "So the Lord changed His mind . . ."
>
> —EXODUS 32:14

Not long after Justin left, I decided to go out dancing alone, to see what it was like. I wanted to act like the girl I'd always wanted to be, long before I'd become the girl I was supposed to be.

Out on the crowded dance floor, I fingered the little black straw in my drink and bounced to the beat, feeling awkward. For a second I startled, thinking I saw Justin. My eyes were still trained to zero in on tan skin and dark hair. But it wasn't him. This guy was taller, his chest and neck wider, his shaved hair coming to a handsome widow's peak. I watched him dance, moving closer. Definitely some nonwhite blood in that boy. Latin maybe. I sipped long and hard on my drink till I pulled up nothing but ice chips and cold air.

Then he noticed me—or at least my halter top—and grinned with warm, clear eyes.

"Is that haircut real?" I screamed over the thrashing 808. "Are you like in the army?"

"Special Forces," he boomed back, and my pupils dilated.

"You're fucking with me," I said, sucking again on the empty straw.

"Scout's honor." He laughed. "Why?"

Oh, my God, not a warrior in a past life but in the present one? There were no words to explain how much this small technicality turned me on. It was very, very promising.

"Nothing. You're gorgeous," I told him, the alcohol now running loose in my blood.

"So are you," he said, reducing me to a puddle.

What started out as respectable dancing rapidly deteriorated, exacerbated by the hard muscles of his upper thigh, which were gently bumping me into total submission. His rhythm was impeccable, his body insane, his smile kind. Before long, I'd fastened myself into a human koala clip.

"Can I kiss you?" he asked as the crowd surged around us. I opened wide for it, like a spoonful of ice cream, and melted into his scent, his face, his sweaty shirt, drooling for more of that sharp pulse from his hips.

"Hang on a sec," he said, starting to wheel around. "I have to find my friends—I don't see them."

He took my hand as if we'd been dating for years, and I followed him outside, past the bouncers and into the parking lot where he paced the empty spaces.

"Shit! I can't believe this," he growled. "They're gone!" My adorable smile petered out. The fun was apparently over. "They're my only way home!"

"Where do you live?" I asked.

"Columbus."

"Columbus?" I managed.

"Fort Benning," he said. "Long way."

"Christ, you really are a soldier. Is there anyone you can call?" I asked. "For a ride?"

He looked at me, exasperated.

"No, I'm from New Hampshire."

"Oh, I'm from Connecticut," I told him, uselessly.

Sobering in the humid night air, I realized that as punishment for being a slut, I'd now end up being a fucking taxi as well. The worst possible ending. "I guess I have to take you, huh."

"I'll pay you," he offered, annoyingly gorgeous even when desperate. "I'm really sorry. I'm going to kick their asses for doing this to me."

No more grinding or kissing, now just silent driving to nowhere, and work in the morning. Christ, it was already the morning. Perfect. Why had I even offered? Why didn't I just ditch him? Not like I was ever going to see this dude again. Argh.

"You drive," I yawned, handing him the keys.

I stared out the window of the passenger seat, disliking the dull ringing in my ears, or the awkward silence that had settled in its place. Gradually the wide, well-lit highway narrowed, and the landscape grew sleepy and dark.

"Don't fall asleep," I warned him.

"No I'm fine."

I nodded in and out, startling awake to check the clock. Four thirty.

"How much longer?" I murmured.

"Halfway."

"Holy shit."

God, I thought. *This is so depressing.*

I thought about all the other Saturday evenings of my life, an infinite succession of denied pleasures, of thwarted fantasies, of finished chores and completed homework. All the bedtimes, like unmarked graves, with me suffocating under the covers as I stared into the darkness and begged my heavenly father to *please make it better*. I'd always done what He wanted me to do. I'd done what Justin wanted me to. I'd done what everyone wanted me to do.

So what did I want to do?

I looked over at this stranger, running my eyes along the striking line of his jaw.

To choose a better ending for once in my life, that's what.

I tasted more of him with my eyes, the way his boxy muscles filled out his shirt, the enticing stretch of his jeans around his hips, his hand on the wheel. Wow, I'd done well. It was an indisputable fact that Mr. Every-Girl's-Fantasy was driving my car.

Why not now?

"I'm sorry about all this," he repeated, feeling my eyes on him. "I really appreciate it."

We reached the barracks as the first light crept into the sky, but for a good fifty miles or so I'd been screwing my courage to the sticking place, letting all the possibilities roll through my mind, each one jockeying for a chance to be heard. Suppose I could do exactly what I wanted to do? Suppose everything I'd been forbidden to do was now fair game?

Do it. Do it now.

Reaching behind my neck, I pulled the string of my shirt and slipped it off, along with the old way of doing things. I looked down at the blue morning light on my topless chest. I felt so mortified. And so alive.

The boy did a double take but did not swerve off the road.

"Those are nice," he said, matter-of-factly.

"Will you fuck me?" I asked, shocking myself.

"Okay," he said, reaching his right hand over to touch me. This shocked me even more. He would? He would!

I breathed, reeling in the avalanche of implications. It was too late to back out now. Oh, no. Oh yes!

In the parking lot outside the entrance, he covered my head with his jacket, and snuck me through a chain-link gate. His arm guiding me, I caught little glimpses of the passing floor tiles as we hurried through a quiet but echoey corridor. Then his roommate was chased out in a flurry of whispers, and he brought me into his room, locked the door and removed my veil.

"We made it?" I asked, laughing nervously.

He nodded and smiled, taking a deep breath, setting my keys on a table. The room was bigger than a dorm, but more austere, more concrete. I had never been in the domain of a real soldier before. For this fact alone I covered him with kisses, moving directly into the re-removal of my top.

I stood nervously at attention as he took off his watch and his shirt, and then began filling his palms with vanilla-scented body lotion. With a half smile, he spread it across my nipples, massaging it in. Slack-jawed, I untied my pants and let them fall off too, hoping he'd rub more there, and anywhere else he wanted. On cue, his hands slid into my thighs, my belly, between my legs, pausing to weaken me with kisses.

Naked, raging wet, and fully moisturized, I rested my butt on the edge of a table and yanked off his belt and jeans, his underwear, teasing his misshapen briefs with the proximity of my parted thighs, running my tongue across the firm plane of his chest, the smooth ridges of his arms, sucking his nipples and his fingers and the shaved hair at the base of his neck. The light coming in the windows was brighter now, and I pulled back to study his face, to take in every inch of him.

"Look at you," I moaned, pained by his beauty. As punishment for being so fucking hot, I knelt down to devour his hard cock, twisting him in my hands, bruising my lips with slow, ferocious strokes, until finally, a decision had to be made whether we'd stop to lay down or just fuck standing up.

"Anywhere," I begged.

He picked me up, straddling my bare body against his waist, his erection threatening below like an angled spear, and laid me down in the shadowy blankets of the bottom bunk, crushing me beneath his weight.

"You have something?" I asked.

"Yeah," he said, rolling over to reach for his pants on the floor, pulling out a crinkly wrapper. He ripped it open and I helped him roll the condom on, grazing him with my tongue as I went, memorizing all the unexpected shapes of his body.

We shifted back into position and I looked up at him, spreading, eager to watch his face as he slid inside me, hoping to see his embattled joy laid bare, the thread of his composure unraveling as he lost control. He pushed into me with a gruff sigh, and I clung to him through the wave of ecstasy, the slow grind, the heroin tide of openmouthed pleasure, and then the rough and insistent battering of his hips as he fought to get more, to hold back. Above the combustion of our bodies, I struggled to quiet my pleading cries, and he tried to steady the bed to keep it from slamming against the wall.

"So good," I warned. *How could it be so good?* The insides of my thighs were trembling, my back arching off the bed. "I think I'm gonna come," I sighed.

"Shh," he reminded me with a smile, offering a pillow to scream into.

"I'm gonna *come*!" I called louder, pushing it aside and pulling his ass deeper, stuffing him into the spiraling pleasure, into a flash of bliss that left me wheezing and drooling into his shoulder, my hips feeding on him, weaning, growing weaker as his pace quickened, his breath raging, hammering me ruthlessly against the cinderblock wall until he convulsed and pulled out, whipping off the condom, coming forcefully all across my chest. I rubbed it into my skin, mixing it with the perfume of sweat and lotion, licking it off my fingertips like honey.

I watched his body heave, his breath slowing, a weary grin on his lips. He fell beside me and for a few suspended moments, we stared at the bunk above us in silence.

"You're my second," I whispered, giggling. "Ever."

"You didn't tell me that," he replied, sounding surprised. As if I was supposed to disclose these things. He considered me, softening.

"Guess what," he said, propping up to touch my hair. "You're my second too. Ever."

And just like that, I was free of the man I was supposed to marry.

I drove home an hour later, wide awake and still trembling, replaying my new collection of secrets. Oh, my God. His balls! His waist! His *dick*. I took a deep, shaky breath. My hands smelled like vanilla and cum, maybe the official scent of the Special Forces.

He had handed me some folded bills on the way out. "Gas money," he'd said. But I was worried that maybe it wasn't, so I'd turned it down flat. As if that would somehow preserve my virtue. Now watching my gas meter ticking on E, I felt pretty stupid.

Still, a one-night stand! A fling! Casual sex with a real live hottie! And I was still alive! For now.

Would there be punishment for exiting the Gates of Purity? Herpes, chlamydia, warts, something bad? But how, since right before he'd unzipped his pants he'd whispered something about how all military guys get tested, that meant he was clean, right? I believed him—how could I not? I had inspected his hard naked penis, right before I ravaged it, and it looked clean.

Clean and healthy and ready to fight for its country.

"God let them go into every sort of sex sin, and let them do whatever they wanted to . . ."

—ROMANS 1:24

Hey," she said in a husky voice, extending her hand like a guy. "Cynthia."

"Hey," I replied, suddenly awash with girly charm. Cynthia was the new chef at the little café where I'd just gotten a job. I wondered if she liked me. After all, I was a girl and she was a lesbian. I didn't know how these things worked exactly. When her back was turned I looked to see if she was checking me out. But nah. She was just putting plates in the window like always. I picked them up and served them to the patio tables.

Sometimes when it got busy I went into the kitchen to help her with the food prep. It was a cramped space and we were always bumping into each other and apologizing.

Cynthia was older, maybe ten years or so, and kind of serious. To me, even the way she chopped celery commanded authority. And I found her body provocative in the most unexpected way. I'd catch myself admiring her hands and

266 | K. Dawn Goodwin

her light-colored eyes. Even in plain cargo pants and a white T-shirt, she had an effortless way of making clothes look good on her long, lean body. And that short, choppy hair, those soft pale lips. Fuck, she looked like a boy. A really hot boy. Only she wasn't. Was I swooning? No.

Wait. Was I? Maybe I was. Holy crap.

What was it? I wondered, as I snuck another glance. I'd always noticed the details of other women's bodies. But never with the understanding that I could *have* their body. Was that what lay at the core of my envy? The desire to secretly fuck them?

After a while, it was more than an accidental bump in the crowded walk-in freezer. It was Cynthia putting her hands on my hips and moving me aside as she was coming through.

" 'Scuse me, darlin'," she'd say, and I'd feel weak in a way that caught me totally off guard. I'd glance at her over my shoulder, and she'd look up in time to see it, and then pretend it hadn't happened.

I liked the way her hair was pushed up in the front, like she'd just run her hand through it. Her T-shirt sleeves were rolled up, James Dean–style, and you could see the edge of a tattoo on her shoulder. Her hands, her gorgeous hands.

I walked up behind her and stood with my chest pressing into her arm, a little too long. Cynthia zoned out, knife paused above a raw zucchini.

"I can't cut straight when you do that, darlin'," she said in a low voice. She went out for a smoke after the lunch rush and I slipped out after her, plucking the cigarette out of her fingers to steal a drag. Her light eyes flashed.

"Come over to my place today, you want to?" she said. "My girlfriend's not home."

"Oh," I said, woozy from the nicotine, or maybe from touching her. "You have a *girlfriend*?"

She looked at me plainly. "Yeah, but not tonight."

That phrase hit me between the eyes, troubling me as much as it turned me on. Doubting seriously that I'd do anything, I found myself racing to get home after work, compelled to shower and shave my body bare. I picked out cute clothes, put on makeup and sat upright on the edge of my bed, watching my reflection in the mirror across the room.

Are you seriously going to go? I asked.

No, of course not.

Then I got in my car and drove straight to her apartment. Cynthia opened the door and greeted me with an evil smile.

A wave of heat rippled through my belly as I walked in.

"What?" She laughed, something I didn't get to see her do very often. She rubbed her forehead with one hand. "Oh, God."

Then she shut the front door behind us and stood there, looking at me. She lifted her hand to move my hair behind my ear. There was a look there, a request for permission as she cocked her head to the side and let me taste her. Her lips and jaw felt small and delicate, her tongue like a girl's, like mine, but her mouth and hands were strong and insistent. She started to pull back, but I reached my hand around her neck and brought her back. My body apparently did not discriminate between boys and girls, not when the kiss crackled like that. I could barely stand upright.

Taking this as a green light, she started undressing me, fondling me, pulling my nipples out of my bra with her mouth. I looked down in fascination as her hands wandered into the waist of my shorts, where I was now as slippery and wet as I'd been for any guy. I took a step backward and wobbled, bringing her down with me onto the white carpeting.

"I've been waiting so long to do this," she said, right before her face disappeared between my thighs, tugging my panties down so she could lick me over and over. I moaned and writhed, the legs of a nearby table going in and out of focus, the heat of her mouth consuming me whole. She was so hungry to get a taste of my overdone girliness, I could feel in my toes how turned-on she was, how much she enjoyed giving me pleasure and seeing me naked. With that, I lost it. I rolled onto my side, blood pulsing in my ears, hair tingling, legs numb.

"Oh, my God," I cried, unable to move. I squinted down at her, trying to focus.

Her shirt was still on, so I figured I needed to get her up to speed. I sat up weakly and kissed her neck, pulling off her shirt, letting her know that I was ready to do it back to her now. And whatever "it" was, I knew with a sinking certainty that I wouldn't know what the hell I was doing.

I cupped the V of her crotch in my hand, making her eyes flutter, stroking and squeezing until she fell back, where I tugged off her pants and underwear. And then, there it was, a pussy. Almost just like my own.

Oh, God.

What, did I think she'd have a dick? I had, kind of. My disappointment defied logic. How exactly did I arrive at this moment? I wondered. And how the hell would I exit it successfully, with my sexual prowess intact? I couldn't possibly top what she'd just done to me.

Easy, I coached myself. *Spastic hand rubbing. Only, use*

your tongue and your neck. Make friction with nonexistent facial muscles, powered by nothing but spit and grit and pure desperation. Suddenly, I had a deep and apologetic appreciation for anyone in the world who had ever gone down on a woman.

I put my mouth on her and tasted her with my tongue, musky and rich, like tasting myself. She whispered my name. But I immediately knew: I was going to suck. I didn't know what to do. Even worse, I lacked the motivation to find out. I couldn't believe it when, after about five minutes or so, I sat up and stopped without explanation.

"I'm sorry," I said, shamefaced. "I'm no good."

"That's fine," she assured me. "You were great."

I looked at her and shook my head, knowing exactly what she meant.

Cynthia still wanted to keep me around, despite my terrible performance and the threat of her live-in girlfriend finding out. We'd leave work together and escape to the dark cool of her apartment, rolling around naked in her bed. She knew how to get my body to react every time, but afterward I was always in a hurry to get up and leave. I had doubts about my ability to be a good lesbian, seeing as how every time she took off her pants, I secretly longed for her dick. For hairy arms and a body that was nothing like mine.

"Stay," she said in a sleepy voice, her gorgeous body twisted in the sheets. "Lie with me awhile. We've got time."

"I gotta go," I said, trying to think of why. I just didn't like the way it felt with her holding me. She needed me in a way I knew she shouldn't. I couldn't reciprocate. And there is nothing so worthless in all the world as a nonreciprocating lover.

"When is your girlfriend coming home?"

"Not till late." She sighed, stretching.

"Still," I said, trying to hook my bra, "it makes me worry."

"She found your hair clip in the sofa cushions." Cynthia grinned. "She was flipping out."

"What did you tell her?"

One thing I was sure of: me and my incriminating pink hair clips did not want to be anywhere near here when two lesbians started throwing dishes at each other. I searched under her bed for my bag.

"I just made up something," Cynthia said. "She bought it, but we've got to be more careful."

"Yeah," I said. "Careful."

But she didn't understand *careful* the same way I did. Careful meant never coming back at all.

When Justin returned from visiting Lesley's hometown, he came over to visit me. I knew by the way he was smiling that he was all better now. In his eyes, the old recording was still on playback: living happily ever after, just the three of us—Justin, me, and whatever past-life lover happened to be in town that weekend.

But I was better too. I was over him.

When he asked what I'd been up to, I told him not too much. Just work, and some jogging, and some sex. Justin's happy face went slack. He staggered back.

"So how was Lesley?" I dared.

"What is happening?" Justin said. "What is happening? What have you *done*?"

We stared hard at each other, and I flashed back to the

time Mom had told me that Grandpa had died. I knew I was supposed to feel sad and cry, but the only thing I could do was laugh. I had run to my room and hid under my blankets so they wouldn't see my demented giggling. It was like that now. I was supposed to be sad, but I wasn't.

"You left to go see her," I said. "You left me. What was I supposed to think?"

"I guess you were supposed to think, hey, hmm, guess I'll go fuck somebody else! Jesus Christ! You knew Lesley was important to me. I thought you understood. But you go and have SEX with some . . . I never fucked Lesley. Never! And you go with somebody you don't even KNOW. Are you fucking joking? You really had sex with him??"

"Yeah," I said. "And also with her."

Justin was shaking his head and backing away from me toward the door. I knew that look. It was heartbreak. It was rage. It was necessary.

We'd done our best to make this thing fit, to make our sex fit, our hearts fit, but they wouldn't anymore.

Predictably, a week later, we tried to see if we could fix everything with a quickie. A consolation fuck. For old times' sake. It hurt a little, as usual, but worse than the pain was the angry look on his face. We got naked in his room and although we'd barebacked for years, he rolled on a condom before going at it, the unspoken need to protect himself from my tainted pussy. *You wrecked it all,* his eyes said, but he was going to try and unwreck it by being a dick, since apparently I liked guys who were dicks. I watched the wall as he pounded me, thinking about Mr. Fort Benning, and about Cynthia, wondering why Justin was still forcing himself to try and love me. Every thrust was hurting him more than me; he had the look of a man who was falling on his sword over and over.

When it was done he lay there and wiped a little dampness from his eyes. I got up to get dressed.

"Are you okay?" I asked.

He turned to me with what looked like pity.

"You're not who I thought you were," he said finally, his voice cracking.

"I know," I replied. "Maybe I've never been."

I liked how that sounded, like a moral victory. It gave me chills.

As I headed out of his door for the last time I looked up at the sky. I was so much smarter now. So much wiser. And more attractive. Men and women everywhere were longing to fuck me—and now they actually could! Neither Justin nor Jesus would stand in their way ever again. The horizon seemed wider somehow, heaven higher, the sunshine brighter. Even God was in a good mood.

Which is why I should've known.

When the Lord is giddy, it can only mean one thing: that the shitstorm of utter dysfunction has only just begun.